Authentic Recipes from
JAMAICA

Recipes and text by John DeMers
Additional essays by Norma Benghiat
Photographs by Eduardo Fuss
Styling by Chia Meow Huay and Christina Ong

With recipes from the following Jamaican restaurants:

Ciboney	Norma at the Wharfhouse
Good Hope	Grand Lido Sans Souci
Grand Lido Negril	Strawberry Hill
Jake's Village	Terra Nova

PERIPLUS EDITIONS
Singapore • Hong Kong • Indonesia

Published by Periplus Editions (HK) Ltd.

www.periplus.com

Copyright © 2005 Periplus Editions (HK) Ltd.
All rights reserved.
ISBN 978-0-7946-0324-3

Distributed by
North America, Latin America and Europe
Tuttle Publishing
364 Innovation Drive, North Clarendon,
VT 05759-9436 U.S.A.
Tel: 1 (802) 773-8930; Fax: 1 (802) 773-6993
info@tuttlepublishing.com
www.tuttlepublishing.com

Japan
Tuttle Publishing
Yaekari Building, 3rd Floor
5-4-12 Osaki, Shinagawa-Ku, Tokyo 141-0032
Tel: (81) 3 5437-0171; Fax: (81) 3 5437-0755
sales@tuttle.co.jp
www.tuttle.co.jp

Asia Pacific
Berkeley Books Pte. Ltd.
3 Kallang Sector #04-01,
Singapore 349278
Tel: (65) 6741 2178; Fax: (65) 6741 2179
inquiries@periplus.com.sg
www.tuttlepublishing.com

All recipes were tested in the Periplus Test Kitchen.

Illustration credits: Detail on front cover is from
"Two Daughters" by Margaret Robson. Photo on
page 11 by Mark Downey. All other photos by
Eduardo Fuss. Ceramic figurines on pages 1, 2, 3 and
15 by Orville Reid. Painting of a Jamaican scene
(endpaper) and painting of a Jamaican kitchen on
page 25 by Fiona Godfrey.

All photos in this book were shot on location in
Jamaica. The publisher would like to thank the follow-
ing hotels and restaurants and their staff who helped
with this project: Terra Nova, Ciboney, Firefly, Good
Hope Plantation Great House, Grand Lido Negril,
Grand Lido Sans Souci, Jake's Village, Norma at the
Wharfhouse and Strawberry Hill.

24 23 22 21   12 11 10 9
Printed in Malaysia   2103TO

Contents

Food in Jamaica

Beneath misty mountain peaks lies a land of infinite complexity

Jamaica is a lush tropical place offering intense adventure amidst one of the most tangled cultures on the face of the earth. It vibrates with the rhythms of reggae, is enlivened by the spices of pepperpot and jerk, and shimmers with the bright colors of flowers and paint. To think of Jamaica is to picture an island paradise of steep, cloud-bedecked mountains and jewel-like blue lagoons—a land of holidays and relaxation. But there is much more to this island.

Jamaica stands out among the islands of the Caribbean for several reasons, first for its sheer size: it is the third largest island in the Caribbean. With an area of more than 4,000 square miles (1,540 square kilometers), Jamaica is one of the few Caribbean islands with extensive agriculture, thus adding depth and variety to its cuisine while liberating its people from subsisting on imported foodstuffs.

The second reason for its uniqueness is the complex ethnic makeup of its people, who came, or were brought to Jamaica because of its vast tracts of tillable soil. Today's Jamaicans are the descendants of the Amerindians, European colonists, African slaves, and those who came later—Irish Indians, Germans, Chinese, Arabs Lebanese and Syrians.

Jamaica's cuisine is the product of this diverse cultural heritage, and its food tells the story of its people. The cuisine's unique flavors include mixtures of tanginess and burning hot chilies, the rich complexity of slowly stewed brown sauces, the spice of intense curries and the cool sweetness of its many tropical fruits. Some of the most authentic examples of the island's food are found in the most humble roadside eateries. And some of its best new fusions can be discovered in the island's hotels and restaurants, prepared by chefs who are joining traditional flavors with new ingredients.

This book aims to unravel Jamaica's multi-faceted culture and make it come alive for you. Whether you have visited often or never, these pages will cast light on the island's history, culture and, most of all, its cuisine. The recipes offered here run the gamut of the island's offerings—from the most humble, but tasty, fried bread to its spiciest jerk chicken.

Perhaps by reading in these pages about Jamaica, you will begin to share the pleasures of this multilayered island paradise, which is as complicated as its stormy history and cultures, as beautiful as its rare wildlife and flowers, and as unforgettable as its easy yet knowing Caribbean smile.

Native Caribbean soil

From its primal beginnings, Jamaica was ripe for harvest. "The fairest land ever eyes beheld," scribbled an eager new arrival in his journal. "The mountains touch the sky." This visitor was hardly the last to be awestruck by Jamaica's beauty, but he was probably the first to write anything down. The year was 1494. The visitor was Christopher Columbus on his second voyage to the New World, and he had come to claim this "fairest land" for God, for himself, and for Spain.

Hardly a set of eyes has settled on these mountains, waterfalls and hills that roll and dive down to the palm-fringed sand, without the beholder thinking he or she was seeing the biblical Garden of Eden. It is important, however, to understand the workings of nature and of humanity that have shaped Jamaica. Known to Jamaica's first residents, the Arawaks, as Xaymaca (land of wood and water), the island was just that before the arrival of Europeans. It featured the two elements in its name—both important to the Arawaks and anyone else hoping to settle here—but little else except a tangle of mangroves. For all the human suffering they brought, the Spanish and British also covered the island with colorful, edible vegetation. The tropical fruits and flowers of this beautiful island are transplants from places such as India, China and Malaysia. Still, nature has been bounteous, offering its many colonists fertile fields in addition to beauty and other resources. The colonizers visited many other Caribbean islands, leaving most of them as spits of sand dotted with a few palm fronds. But in Jamaica they stayed, shaping the island to their own image.

Located in the western Caribbean, Jamaica is larger than all but Cuba and Hispaniola. Millions of years ago the island was volcanic. The mountains that soar to nearly 7,500 feet (2,250 meters) are higher than any in the eastern half of North America. These peaks run through the center of Jamaica. The island has a narrow coastal plain, no fewer

ABOVE: The Spanish and British exported colorful and delicious food products from Jamaica with the help of thousands of slaves brought in from West Africa, the ancestors of today's Jamaicans. RIGHT: A typical island breakfast of Run Down (recipe page 48), boiled green bananas and potatoes.

than 160 rivers, and a dramatic coastline of sand coves. Much of Jamaica is limestone, which explains the profusion of underground caves and offshore reefs—not to mention the safe and naturally filtered drinking water that first impressed the Arawaks. In the mountains of the east (the highest, Blue Mountain Peak, rises to 7359 feet (2,243 meters) misty pine forests and Northern Hemisphere flowers abound. Homes there actually have fireplaces, and sweaters are slipped on in the evenings. In places, the mountains plunge down to the coast creating dramatic cliffs. The hotter, flatter southern coast can look like an African savanna or an Indian plain, with alternating black and white beaches and rich mineral springs. There are tropical rain forests next to peacefully rolling and brilliantly green countryside that, save for the occasional coconut palm, could be the south of England. It is surely one of history's quirks: many parts of Jamaica (a small place by the world's standards) resemble the larger countries from which so much of its population hails.

In the heyday of the British Empire, flowering and fruit trees were brought from Asia, the Pacific and Africa; evergreens came from Canada to turn the cool slopes green; and roses and nasturtiums came from England. The ackee, which is so popular for breakfast, came from West Africa on the slave ships. Breadfruit was first brought from Tahiti by no less a figure than Captain Bligh of the Bounty. Sugarcane, bananas and citrus fruits were introduced by the Europeans.

Jamaica did send out a few treasures. One of the island's rare native fruits, the pineapple, was sent to a faraway cluster of islands known as Hawaii. Its mahogany was transplanted to Central America. There are varieties of orchids, bromeliads and ferns that are native only to Jamaica, not to mention the imported fruits like the Bombay mango that seem to flourish nowhere else in this hemisphere.

The island is clearly a paradise if you are a bird, simply based on the number of exotics that call it home. Native and migratory, these range from the tiny bee hummingbird to its long-tailed cousin, the "doctor bird", to the mysterious solitaire with its mournful cry. Visitors to Jamaica's north coast become acquainted with the shiny black Antillean grackle known as kling-kling, as it gracefully shares their breakfast toast. And those hiking through the high mountains can catch a glimpse of *Papillo homerus*, one of the world's largest butterflies. Unlike most of the population, animal or human, *Papillo homerus* is a native.

A tropical climate prevails in Jamaica's coastal lowlands, with an annual mean temperature of about 80 degrees Fahrenheit (27 degrees Celsius). Yet the heat and humidity are moderated by northeastern trade winds that hold the average to about 72°F (22°C) at elevations of 2,950 feet (894 meters). Rainfall varies widely around the island, from a mere 32 inches (80 centimeters) annually in the vicinity of Kingston to more than 200 inches (500 centimeters) in the mountains in the northeast. The rainiest months are May, June, October and November with hurricane season hitting the island in the late summer and early autumn.

The Jamaican economy relies heavily on agriculture, though the island is blessed with mineral deposits of bauxite, gypsum, lead and salt—the bauxite constituting one of the largest deposits in the world. Despite its significant diversification into mining, manufacturing and tourism, the island continues to struggle against a budget deficit each

year. Agriculture still employs more than 20 percent of the Jamaican population. While sugarcane is clearly the leading crop, other principal agricultural products include bananas, citrus fruits, tobacco, cacao, coffee, coconuts, corn, hay, chilies, ginger, mangoes, potatoes and arrowroot. The livestock population includes some 300,000 cattle, 440,000 goats, and 250,000 pigs.

This is the lush backdrop to life on a Caribbean island. Of course, no profile of Jamaica would be complete without a description of its single most unforgettable resource: its people.

Out of many, one nation

Listen closely in Jamaica and you will hear a thousand references from well beyond this Caribbean island. Jamaicans speak of places in England and in Israel—from Somerset to Siloah, Highgate to Horeb—except that these places are in Jamaica, too. And hopping aboard a bus, you will encounter Arawak place names such as Liguanea, Spanish names such as Oracabessa, and entirely Jamaican flips such as Red Gal Ring and even Me-No-Sen You-No-Come.

These place names reveal the country's many influences, and, indeed, Jamaica's 2.3 million people form a spectrum of races that would give the most dedicated genealogist a migraine. Most people are black, or some shade of brown, but many have undertones of Chinese, East Indian, Middle Eastern (known on the island as Syrian, no matter what their origin) and European. Five centuries after Columbus, the rainbow of natural colors in Jamaica's landscape is still vibrant. And there is no better metaphor than this rainbow for the mix of Jamaica's cultures. With its tension and its

tolerance, this island is truly one of the globe's most fascinating ethnic environments.

The first of many peoples known to hit the beaches of Jamaica did so about a thousand years after the death of Christ. Amerindians paddled their canoes over from the Orinoco region of South America. Before that, there is the possibility that a more primitive group, the Ciboneys, spent some time here on their trek from Florida to other large Caribbean islands. The Arawaks, however, left their imprint on Jamaica.

When Christopher Columbus stepped ashore in 1494, the island had already served as the Arawaks' home for nearly five hundred years. They were, by all accounts, gentle folk. Their way of life included hunting, fishing, farming and dancing their way through a calendar of festivals. The Spanish, however, had other plans, forcing them into hard labor and killing the last of them within 50 years. Once they had Jamaica to themselves, the Spanish seemed to decide they didn't really want it. Their searches of the interior turned up no quick-profit precious metals, so they let the land fester in poverty for 161 years. When 5000 British soldiers and sailors appeared in Kingston harbor in 1655, the Spanish just fled.

The next three centuries under British rule provided Jamaica with its genteel underpinnings and the rousing

OPPOSITE: A late nineteenth-century print of Muirton House and Plantation Morant Bay shows Jamaica's lush vegetation and agricultural bounty. ABOVE: Despite branching into mining and manufacturing, agriculture and plantation life is still a vital part of the Jamaican lifestyle.

pirate tradition that enlivens this period of Caribbean history. British buccaneer Henry Morgan was close friends with Jamaica's governor and enjoyed the protection of His Majesty's government no matter what he chose to plunder.

The notorious Port Royal (known as the Wickedest City in Christendom) grew on a spit of land across from present-day Kingston. Morgan and his brigands found a haven there where ships could be repaired and loot could be spent. Morgan enjoyed a prosperous life. He was actually knighted and appointed Lieutenant Governor of Jamaica before the age of 30. Port Royal, however, did not fare so well. On June 7, 1692, an earthquake tipped most of the city into the sea, and a tidal wave wiped out whatever was left. Port Royal disappeared. Recently, divers have turned up some of the treasure, but most of it still waits in the murky depths.

The eighteenth century was prosperous for Jamaica's sugar barons, who ruled as undisputed masters of their British plantations. The island became the largest sugar-producing colony on earth, mostly through the sweat of African slaves. Magnificent residences known as "great houses" rose above the cane fields. Fortunes built on sugar were the envy of even Britain's king, giving rise to the expression "rich as a West Indian planter."

Such words, of course, had little meaning for the 2 million slaves brought from Africa to Jamaica and Barbados. The slaves were cruelly used and were forbidden to speak their own languages or practice their own customs. Discipline was harsh, but the slave owners could never quite quell the spirit of rebellion that existed. Jamaica has a long history of slave uprisings and of slave violence against tyrannical planters.

For the slaves, there was also the ever-present inspiration of the Maroons, descendants of escaped slaves from Spanish days. Called *cimarrones* (runaways) by the Spaniards, these men and women lived in the mountains, defying and out-witting British troops at every turn. The Maroons drew other runaways and staged rebellions until a treaty in 1739 gave them a measure of autonomy that they retain to this day.

As it turns out, the planters proved almost as rebellious as their slaves. When the thirteen American colonies declared their independence from Britain, the Jamaica House of Assembly voted to join them. This declaration never quite took hold in world politics, but it was considered a daring gesture all the same. As with cotton in the American South, the entire sugar system proved less profitable when the slave trade was abolished in Jamaica in 1807 and slavery itself ended in 1838. The transition was peaceful compared to the Civil War that divided the United States. The planters' initial plan was to hire former slaves who knew how to handle each job. But the British quickly discovered that most free men wanted nothing more to do with plantations. So a frenzied effort was launched to attract cheap labor from abroad, initiating Jamaica's great age of immigration.

Workers came in ethnic waves over the decades. As each group rose from the lowest levels of the social system, another group had to be solicited to do the island's dirty work. Small numbers of Germans and Irish came first, then workers from India and China followed in great numbers.

A full 95 percent of Jamaica's people trace their heritage to Africa, yet most have some link or distant relative tying them to Britain, the Middle East, China, Portugal, Germany, South America or another island in the Caribbean. In general, these groups live together peacefully—partially because they've had to over the years to survive and partially because there has been so much intermarriage.

By the mid 1900s, a "national identity" had supplanted a British one in the hearts and minds of Jamaicans. This new identity was given official recognition on August 6, 1962, when Jamaica became an independent nation with only loose ties to the Commonwealth. On that day, the Union Jack was lowered for the last time, and the new black, green and gold Jamaican flag was lifted up.

"Out of many, one nation" is the motto of Jamaica, though it struggles today with the same problems that plague so many Caribbean islands. Its unity can be heard in the language of its people, which carries both words and word patterns from West African languages. And when Jamaicans speak, even in dark moments, it is with a unique lilt that makes every sentence a song.

The Rastafarians

The tremendous mingling of cultures in Jamaica has also led to a mingling of religions. The vast majority of Jamaicans consider themselves Christian, yet there are significant communities of Jews, Hindus, Muslims and other religions. But Rastafarianism is the religion that was born in Jamaica, and it commands a serious following on the island—along with the respect of even those Jamaicans who choose not to follow it.

Say the word "Rasta" and an image of marijuana-smoking reggae musicians comes to mind, for reggae is the best-known product of this religion, spread through the world as it has been by such famous reggae musicians as Bob Marley, who closely associated reggae with Rastafarianism.

The Rastafarian religion or movement is a significant phenomena to emerge out of Jamaica's plantation slave society. It was born of the need to counteract the denigration of people of African descent in a society that gave little recognition to the majority of its citizens. The Rastafarians withdrew from "Babylon" or Western society and created their own music, speech, beliefs, cuisine, lifestyle and attire.

Rastas believe in the deity of the late Ethiopian king, Haile Selassie, who was the messiah, Rastafari. They believe in repatriation to Ethiopia and consider themselves to be one of the tribes of Israel. Rastafarians believe that certain Old Testament chapters speak about Haile Selassie and Ethiopia. "Jah," or God, is seen as a black man. The Rastas see themselves as the true Hebrews, chosen by "Jah." Right-living Rastas are considered to be saints, and the others are called "brethren."

The Rastafarian religion has a code against greed, dishonesty and exploitation. Except for the sacramental smoking of ganja (marijuana, the possession, sale and use of which are illegal in Jamaica), true Rastas are law-abiding, have strong pride in black history, a positive self-image, and strive for self-sufficiency. The Rasta lifestyle reflects these beliefs.

Some orthodox Rastas resemble biblical figures, bearded and garbed in long robes, carrying staffs and covering

their dreadlocks with turbans. Rastas quote Leviticus 21.5: "They shall not make baldness upon their head, neither shall they shave off the corners of their beard, nor make any cuttings in their flesh" as the reason for wearing dreadlocks, which are formed by leaving hair to grow naturally without combing. The longer the dreadlocks, the longer the Rasta's devotion to the holy ways of living. Many Rastas wear dreadlocks wrapped neatly in turbans, and this is the only outward sign of their religion. They incorporate the colors of the Ethiopian flag, red, green and gold, into all kinds of clothing.

The Rastas' diet, called I-tal (which means "natural" in the Rasta language), is essentially a strict vegetarian one. They believe that man should eat only that which grows from the soil. Food should not include the dead flesh of any living animal, and pork is strictly omitted. This diet also excludes manufactured food of any kind because it contains additives, which Rastas believe cause illnesses, such as cancer. In addition, the foods they eat are grown naturally, without the use of any artificial fertilizers.

I-tal cooking uses the produce of the land—peas, beans and a variety of other vegetables, starches and fruits that are locally available. While some Rastas will eat fish, chicken and I-tal food, others will eat only I-tal food in its raw state. Ganja is often included in cooked foods, and

OPPOSITE: Enjoy a delicious lunch featuring the local seafood in the calm and serene surroundings of Jake's Village, a picturesque hotel on Jamaica's southwestern coast. ABOVE: This Rastafarian, selling Caribbean lobster near Buff Bay, grows a beard and dreadlocks to demonstrate his pact with Jah (God). The Rastafarian religious movement grew out of Jamaica's slave society.

infusions are taken for medicinal purposes. Rastas abstain from spirits, beer and wine. Instead they drink fruit juices that are mixed to create non-alcoholic I-tal drinks.

Some Rastas do not use silverware or plates. Instead, they eat from coconut-shell and calabash bowls with their fingers. This, they say, identifies them with their African roots. Some Rastas go so far as to refuse to drink processed water and instead collect rain water to use in the preparation of their food.

"Groundlings," or gatherings, are held at specific times to celebrate the birthday of Haile Selassie or the Ethiopian Christmas and New Year. At these gatherings *niyabinga* drums and Rastafarian music create an intense spiritual mood.

Ganja, which most likely came to Jamaica with the East Indians, plays an important role in the lives of Rastas. Ganja is smoked in cone-shaped "spliffs" made from brown paper bags or newspaper, or in a bamboo chillum pipe that is passed around by members. Rastas smoke the herb to inspire open conversation.

The Rastas have developed their own dialect by replacing the "me" in the Jamaican Creole language with "I and I," in order to insert a positive notion of self into their speech. For example, "me have mi table" is changed to "I and I have mi table."

Vibrant colors are the hallmark of Rastafarian art, and its influence can be seen in the works of traditional artists such as Parboosingh, as well as in ceramics, the theater and dance. The profound influence the Rastas have had on indigenous musical forms is well known, from ska to rock steady to the most significant phenomenon, reggae. The latter, with its hypnotic beat and protest lyrics, has created an artistic form that has taken on a life of its own and carried the spirit of Rastafarianism throughout the world.

From the fields to the table

It might have been the climate and fertility that first brought the Amerindians to Jamaica, but it was the search for gold that brought the Europeans. When this search failed, they turned to the island's other resources. Crops that were brought to Jamaica from far away have flourished here as in no other place.

In the days of the great plantations, many slaves were allowed to grow their own vegetables in tiny plots around their huts—though animal husbandry was, for the most part, forbidden. There was a superstition that slaves allowed to eat red meat would develop a taste for their masters. Small-time agriculture, however, prospered in this way, producing a surplus the slaves were encouraged to sell among themselves. This produced the Jamaican tradition of Sunday as market day—a swirling scene in the center of a town, the air alive with shouts of higglers (street vendors) hawking their wares.

LEFT AND RIGHT: Peddlers or higglers, like the ones pictured, are usually female, a tradition that has predominated since it was brought over from West Africa during the colonial period.

Jamaican markets were the social gathering place for country folk to meet to gossip and exchange news. Both the buyers and the sellers came together to partake in this weekly event, which could be likened to a country fair. In those days, the country folk would set out very early in the morning, or often the day before, with their donkeys laden with produce. Drays drawn by mules would create a mighty traffic jam as they weaved through the throng of people.

Inside and outside the market there would be an abundance of colorful fruits and vegetables—red tomatoes, mangoes and papayas; purple egplants; a green abundance of cho-chos and callaloo; bunches of green and ripe bananas, breadfruits and plantains—all arranged to catch the eye of the passerby.

Part of the noise and bustle were the loud cries of the higglers, who, as Martha Beckwith wrote in *Black Roadways*, "had their own musical cry which rises and falls with a peculiar inflection.

"Buy yu' white yam! Buy yu' yellow yam! Buy yu' green bananas! Ripe pear fe breakfast—ripe pear!"

Not many itinerant vendors are to be found in towns today. The higglers have established themselves in market stalls and now often sell on the roadsides, asking prices that are higher than those in the supermarket. The produce they carry, however, is usually of superior quality.

Today's markets have changed with the times; very rarely are donkeys and carts used for transportation. The market people now arrive via bus, truck or van. There are rarely live

chickens for sale. Markets are not as vibrant as they were in the pre-supermarket days, but the market is still the place to find the widest selection of fresh produce.

Much of the vegetables and fruits in Jamaica are grown by small farmers. There are very few large fruit orchards. Instead small farmers mix their fruit trees with vegetables so that the standard Jamaican backyard is thickly planted with mangoes, limes, sweet and sour sops, ackees, sugarcane, bananas, avocados and whatever else the land will hold.

Vegetables are grown both in the cooler mountains and on the plains. The Santa Cruz area of St. Elizabeth is known as the breadbasket of Jamaica. The industrious farmers here manage to produce an abundance of food, in spite of a lack of irrigation, through heavy mulching, which helps the soil retain moisture. The largest quantities of spring onions, thyme and onions are grown in this area. The mountain regions produce excellent lettuce, bok choy, cabbage, spring onions and thyme.

Starches and root crops consisting of breadfruit, cassava (bitter and sweet), sweet and Irish potatoes, cocos, yams, plantains and bananas both ripe and green—the latter being eaten as a starch—are grown both in the mountains and on the plains.

The island is blessed with an astonishing variety of fruits—some indigenous, others introduced over the centuries. Summer is, of course, the most abundant season for fruits such as pineapples, mangoes, otaheiti apples, sweet and sour sops, plums, naseberries and so on.

Both dairy and beef cattle are raised in Jamaica. Beef cattle were usually bred by owners of large sugar estates and other landowners who had enough acreage of pangola grass to support the cattle. Pigs were introduced into Jamaica as early as the sixteenth century by the Spaniards and became wild in the mountains. They were notably hunted and barbecued, or "jerked," by the Maroons, using a method that was uniquely their own. Originally, goats were reared by the peasantry strictly for their milk. However, with the influx of Indian immigrants, the demand for goat meat has escalated to such an extent that it often more expensive than beef. Poultry was introduced in waves to the island by the Spaniards, the British, and the Africans. Many households also raise chickens on a small scale.

Fish and crustaceans were once abundant but have become scarce to overfishing. They now come mainly from the Pedro Banks to the south of the island, and commercially produced pond fish now fill the demand for wild fish.

The astonishing array of ingredients available on the island has been the source of inspiration for many a newcomer to Jamaica who, eager to re-create recipes from home, has created new dishes that are at the root of today's Jamaican cuisine.

—*John DeMers and Norma Benghiat*

BELOW: Collecting, transporting and counting bunches of bananas to fill the cargo holds of boats destined for North America. On the return trip the boats were filled with a very different sort of cargo—tourists escaping the bleak northern winter. OPPOSITE: Jerk is Jamaica's national dish.

A Diversity of Cooking Styles

Goat feeds and wedding cakes—new traditions displace the old

Jamaica's cuisine has changed over time, and new traditions have displaced some of the old. But eating customs and dishes exist there today that are both remnants of Jamaica's colonial history and the result of its many immigrant traditions.

One cannot say enough about the influence of immigration on the food of Jamaica. Since the British had already acquired a craving for curry in India, Indians found a ready audience for their contributions to the great Jamaican cook pot. They brought from home the technique for blending fragrant curry powders and using them to showcase local meat and fish. When traditional lamb proved hard to find, they drafted the most convenient substitute. The dish curried goat was born, turning up now and again with a side of chow mein.

The Chinese and, in smaller numbers, the Syrians and Lebanese added tremendous complexity to Jamaica's culture and cuisine. The island's very old Jewish community was joined over time by migrant Arab traders from Palestine. These groups all prepared traditional dishes from their homes—curried goat and sweet and sour pork, to name a few of the many—that have become an integral part of Jamaica's cuisine.

Eating traditions hark back to the days of Britain's control of the island. During the eighteenth century on the plantations meals were copious for the residents of the grand plantation houses. The day began with a cup of coffee, chocolate or an infusion of some local herb, all equally called "tea." Breakfast was served later in the morning, a "second breakfast" was served at noon, and dinner was served in the late afternoon or evening. Both the breakfast and "second breakfast" were substantial meals, as was dinner.

Today's Jamaican breakfast varies considerably depending on where one lives. Farmers, who rise early to tend their fields, start the day with a cup of "tea." Late in the morning they may eat a substantial breakfast of callaloo and saltfish (salted cod) or, ackee and saltfish accompanied with yams, roasted breadfruit, dumplings or green bananas.

Both country and town lunches consist of some of the favorite Jamaican dishes, such as stewed peas (which are what Jamaicans call beans); curried goat; oxtail; escoveitched fish (marinated in lime juice), brown stewed fish (pan-fried and then braised in a brown sauce seasoned with chilies and spices) or simply fried fish. These main dishes are usually served with rice, yams, green bananas or other starches. There might also be a satisfying soup of meat, vegetables, yams, cocos (taro, also called dasheen) and dumplings served as a one-pot meal. Dinner can include stewed beef, jerked meat, oxtail and beans, fish or fricasseed chicken.

The most important meal of every Jamaican household is the traditional Sunday dinner. This is usually eaten midafternoon after eating a bigger Sunday breakfast of ackee and saltfish or liver and onions with johnnycakes, green bananas and bammie (a flat cassava bread) and fruit.

Dinner (sometimes called late lunch as well) is the time when family and friends gather for a more relaxed meal. Rice and peas are de rigueur for Sundays, and often at least two meats—fricasseed chicken as well as a very spicy roast beef—will be served. Fried plantains, string beans, carrots and a salad might accompany the meats, followed by a pudding, cake or fruit salad. Beverages include soft drinks, lemonade, coconut water, beer and rum or rum punch.

Christmas is the most important holiday of the year for Jamaicans. This goes back to the days of slavery when there were four seasonal holidays—Christmas, Easter or Picanny Christmas, Crop over Harvest and the Yam Festival. The Yam Festival has since disappeared, but the other three holidays are still celebrated, and celebrated well.

During the eighteenth and nineteenth centuries, Christmas consisted of three nonconsecutive days—Christmas, Boxing and New Year's days. During this time, a temporary metamorphosis occurred in the relationship between master and slaves: the slaves assumed names of prominent whites, richly dressed (most of their savings went into dressing), and addressed their masters as equals. Christmas celebrations began early in the morning when a chorus of slaves visited the great house, singing "good morning to your nightcap and health to the master and mistress." After this, the

slaves collected extra rations of salted meats for the three days of celebrations.

The great attraction on Boxing Day was the John Canoe Dance—which is slowly dying out—and on New Year's Day, the great procession of the Blue and Red Set Girls. Each set gave a ball, and each was represented by a king and queen. The queen and her attendants wore lavish gowns that were kept secret until the day of their appearance.

For most Jamaicans today, the idea of Christmas conjures up cool days, shopping, social gatherings, and much eating and drinking. This is the time of year when the sorrel plant, used to make the traditional red Christmas drink, is in season along with the fresh gungo (pigeon) peas used to make Christmas rice and peas. A very rich plum pudding, made from dried fruits soaked for weeks in rum and port, is a must for Christmas dinner. It is usually served with a "hard" or brandy sauce.

Easter time reflects the passing of the cooler months and heralds the coming of summer. For strict Catholics, it means the abandoning of meats for fish. Even though the majority of the Jamaican population is not Catholic, more fish is eaten during Lent than at any other time of the year.

The eating of buns and cheese during Easter is a truly Jamaican innovation. Buns of every description are baked and eaten in large quantities—especially as a snack with a piece of cheese. Each bakery vies with the next to produce the best buns. But the buns of yesteryear, most of which were baked by small bakeries, were much tastier than today's. Now the large bakeries make most of the buns, and at times the raisins and currants are hardly visible except as decorations.

Jamaican weddings today have become much like those in the West. But of more interest were the old country weddings, celebrated grandly and often attended by the whole village. They were preceded by many nights of preparation, usually consisting of ring games. A feed was held the night before the wedding for the groom. This consisted of curried ram goat and sometimes "dip and fall back," a dish of salted shad cooked in coconut milk and served with a lot of rum. It is said that the goat's testicles were roasted and served to the groom. These days, Mannish Water, a stew made of a goat's organs and head is served to grooms the night before the wedding to increase virility.

The day before the wedding a procession of young girls, all dressed in white, carried the wedding cakes on their heads to the bride's house. The main cakes were in the form of pyramids, and each cake was covered with a white veil. The picturesque custom of young girls carrying the cakes on their heads has almost disappeared as transportation by cars is now used more often.

The wedding feast differed from village to village, but usually it consisted of a huge meal of roast pig, curried goat and traditional side dishes. The Sunday following the celebrations, the couple attended church with members of the wedding party.

While these traditions are slipping away, the flavors of the past are alive and well in Jamaica.

The joys of jerk

Jerk—the fiery food that is now popular all over the globe—is truly a part of Jamaica's history. From M.G. Lewis in 1834 to Zora Neale Hurston in 1939, chroniclers of the West Indies tell us of their flavorful encounters with the Maroons—and with the Maroons' favorite food, a spice and pepper-encrusted slow-smoked pork called "jerk." The Maroons, escaped slaves living in Jamaica's jungle interior, developed many survival techniques—but none more impressive than the way they hunted wild pigs, cleaned them between run-ins with the law, covered them with a mysterious spice paste and cooked them over an aromatic wood fire.

Lewis gives us a vivid picture of a Maroon dinner of land tortoise and barbecued pig: "two of the best and richest dishes that I ever tasted, the latter in particular, which was dressed in the true Maroon fashion, being placed on a barbecue, through whose interstices the steam can ascend, filled with peppers and spices of the highest flavor, wrapped in plantain leaves and then buried in a hole filled with hot stones by whose vapor it is baked, no particle of juice being thus suffered to evaporate."

Even more exciting is Hurston's description a century later of an actual hunting expedition with the Maroons. As an anthropologist, she was trained to discern cultural and ethnic truths. But in one extended passage, what she discovers is the unforgettable flavor of jerk pork.

"All of the bones were removed, seasoned and dried over the fire to cook. Towards morning we ate our fill of jerked pork. It is more delicious than our American barbe-

cue. It is hard to imagine anything better than pork the way the Maroons jerk it. When we had eaten all that we could, the rest was packed up with the bones and we started the long trek back to Accompong."

Thanks to Americans who have followed in Hurston's footsteps, the jerk-scented "trek back to Accompong" has never ended. The Maroon method of cooking and preserving pork has become a Jamaican national treasure, inspiring commercial spice mixes, bottled marinades and the use of the word "jerk" around the world.

The word "jerk" itself, as with so many in Jamaica, is something of a mystery. Most Jamaicans offer the non-scholarly explanation that the word refers to the jerking motion either in turning the meat over the coals or in chopping off hunks for customers. Still, there is a more serious explanation.

"Jerk," writes F. G. Cassidy (who penned the *Dictionary of Jamaican English* published in London in 1961), "is the English form of a Spanish word of Indian origin." This process of linguistic absorption is so common in the Caribbean that it is persuasive here. Cassidy says that the original Indian word meant to prepare pork in the manner of the Quichua Indians of South America. Thus, jerking was learned from the Indians, either the Arawaks or others from across the Caribbean, and preserved by the Maroons. There's also an undeniable link to the Dutch word *gherken*, meaning "to pickle or marinate."

Until recently, jerk remained a dish made with pork, true to its roots. Now roadside pits and "jerk centers" dish up chicken, fish, shrimp—even lobster. Until recently, jerk was found only in parts of Jamaica with strong Maroon traditions,

including the interior known as Cockpit Country and a tiny slice of Portland on the northeast coast at Boston Bay. Now jerk is sold everywhere, and its irresistible scent, which impressed Lewis and Hurston in their day, fills the air.

Several of the best jerk purveyors are still on the beach at Boston Bay, somewhat off the tourist track and therefore frequented by Jamaicans. These eateries are little more than thatch-roofed huts built over low-lying, smoldering fires. On top of these fires you'll often find sheets of tin, blown off some roof in a storm, that are used as griddles. The meat is cooked on these sheets, covered with plantain leaves.

The jerk sellers tend to be characters with colorful nicknames and singsong sales pitches that tell you why their jerk is the best on the island. If you don't believe them, they'll pull out glass jars of their jerk paste, warn you it's lethal with Scotch Bonnet chilies, and scoop some out for a tasting on the spot. They'll even be delighted to sell you a Red Stripe to cool down your flaming taste buds.

—*John DeMers and Norma Benghiat*

OPPOSITE: A cook serves up jerk at Faith's Pen—a lively collection of fast-food stalls along the highway that crosses the island between Ocho Rios and Kingston. ABOVE: Roadside pits and "jerk centers" whip up a spread of jerk dishes to include chicken, fish, and even lobster jerk.

Jamaican Coffee and Rum

Two world-renowned island beverages

Rum, the wild firewater of slaves and buccaneers, is the spirit of Jamaica. As an industry it is more important to Jamaica's economy now than sugar—even though sugar producers failed to notice its value for the longest time.

No one is certain how rum got its name, but it may be a short version of sugar's botanical name, *Saccharum officinarum*. According to one story the name derives from "rumbustion" or "rumbullion," archaic English words meaning "uproar" or "rumpus."

The process of refining sugar from raw cane produces a by-product of juice and molasses. In sugar's heyday, this by-product was sometimes given to slaves or to livestock. Sometimes it was simply tossed out. Finally, someone noticed that a chemical change was occurring in the by-product. All the heat and natural yeast in the island air spontaneously brought about fermentation. According to Jamaican legend, an extremely thirsty slave dipped a ladle into a trash pool and emerged from the experience a good deal happier than he had been before. Before long, plantation owners were building distilleries alongside their sugar refineries.

By the nineteenth century, when the emancipation of slaves made sugar less profitable, rum remained a high-profit item and was produced everywhere. There were 148 distilleries in Jamaica in 1893. Today, 4.5 million gallons of rum are produced on the island each year. Some of the best-known brands are Appleton, Gold Label and Myers.

The production of rum, then and now, involves three stages: fermentation, distillation and aging. Water and yeast are added to molasses and allowed to ferment. Distillation produces a colorless liquid: dark rums are sometimes enriched with "dunder," solid matter left in the still from previous batches.

Traditionally, Jamaican rum was stored in oak casks for three to twenty years, depending on the type of rum and the bouquet desired. A light amber color is imparted by the oak; caramel is added to give the rum a darker color. These days, huge stainless steel vats are replacing the oak casks, and the aging process is being shortened to one to three years. Twenty-year-old rum, a rarity, is looked upon with the same esteem in Jamaica as a good cognac in France.

That said, it follows that this liquid has a special mystique around the island. It is widely imbibed for its medicinal properties, and islanders use it as a rub to treat fevers and prevent colds. Beyond that, rum is used ritually when you add a room to your house in Jamaica. You simply must sprinkle it over the area to be enclosed to ward off spirits or the dreaded evil eye.

Blue Mountain bounty

"Blue Mountain coffee, the most delicious in the world . . ." Those words were not spoken by some highly paid spokesperson for the Jamaican coffee industry but by Agent 007 himself—world-class spy James Bond.

Bond author Ian Fleming, who lived a great part of the year in a house called Goldeneye outside Ocho Rios, no doubt developed a taste for Blue Mountain before it became the world's most expensive coffee. Actually, Bond's statement sounds a little overblown to connoisseurs of coffee, but that is strictly a matter of taste. Blue Mountain's light, almost tea-like subtlety sets it apart from the more robust and full-bodied brews of Kenya or Sumatra.

As much as it might like to be, Jamaica is not the birthplace of coffee. Louis XV of France sent three plants to Martinique in 1723, and only one survived the trip despite incredible pampering. Five years later, the Jamaican governor, Sir Nicholas Lawes, brought seedlings from Martinique and planted them just outside Kingston. The government supported coffee cultivation in the hope of easing the economy's dependence on sugar. The industry grew slowly, century to century, only to be virtually wiped out by a hurricane in 1951. Happily, one Victor Munn had a tiny 5-acre (2-hectare) plot at Mavis Bank in the Blue Mountain foothills. He set up a small factory and was able to process his coffee, as well as that from the few remaining estates.

Jamaica has limited coffee acreage—and limits within that as to what can be sold as Blue Mountain coffee. Only a tiny section of the island between Kingston and Port Antonio features the perpetual cool mist and the well-drained peaks of volcanic loam required to produce these

beans at their best. Of Jamaica's 28,000 acres (11,000 hectares) of coffee, a mere 9,000 acres (3,600 hectares) are within the official Blue Mountain region. There, above 2,000 feet (610 meters), Jamaican growers germinate their Arabica seeds for one to two years, then cut off one of the two root systems before planting. It's a lengthy five years before the first harvest, yet clearly (given its price) Blue Mountain is worth the wait.

The harvest itself is slow and labor-intensive. The job is done by hand: When the beans are red and at their peak of ripeness, they are picked one at a time. They are then carried down the mountain by men or mules and processed at ramshackle coffee stations that are very humble in comparison to their finished product. The beans are sorted, and the outer pulp is removed from the inner beans, which are then dried, husked, and roasted.

In the middle of the nineteenth century, Britain instituted a new trade policy under which Jamaican coffee growers lost their protected trade status. Small Jamaican coffee growers were nearly wiped out by having to compete with coffee growers from South America.

By 1973, the coffee market had grown again to the point that some government control was required. Almost any coffee grown, processed or even vacationing in Jamaica was sold (and, of course, priced) as Blue Mountain. Yet the quality was not always there. To change this, the government issued a decree that only coffee grown in a specific region and processed by one of four estates (Mavis Bank, Silver Hill, Moy Hall and the Government Station at Wallenford) could be labeled 100 percent Blue Mountain coffee. Any other Jamaican coffee would be graded as Blended Blue Mountain (20 percent expensive beans), High Mountain Blend, or Lowland coffee.

It is the Japanese who deserve the credit, or the blame, for the fame (and high prices) of the best Blue Mountain coffee. Japanese investors bought large parcels of coffee-growing land in Jamaica in the early 1980s. This brought an infusion of money into the industry, but it is also why so much Jamaican coffee goes directly to Japan. About 80 percent of all beans from these mountains are exported there, where the coffee sells not for US$30 per kilo but for US$15 per brewed cup. And brewed coffee is more than 99 percent water!

With the Japanese hold on the market, most Blue Mountain coffee has been shipped to Japan first and then resold to buyers elsewhere. Markups tend to be significant, as does a certain mystique. In the end, it's the law of supply and demand that pushes prices above US$60 per kilo, and sometimes as high as US$50. Happily for growers in the Blue Mountains, there are many coffee addicts who swear they will drink no other brew.

—John DeMers

OPPOSITE: Enjoy a cuppa of the local brew at Firefly, the home of British playwright Noel Coward, with its magnificent view overlooking Bloody Bay beach at Post Antonio. Firefly is now a museum and open to the public. ABOVE: Coffee from Mavis Bank Central Factory, an old-fashioned coffee grinder and a stunning view of the mountains from the resort at Strawberry Hill. Mavis Bank is one of four pulperies, or processing plants, that process all the beans from the Blue Mountains.

The Jamaican Kitchen

From traditional to modern, this kitchen serves up simple and celebratory food

There are Jamaican kitchens so traditional that they seem like historic re-creations—and others so modern they look no different from those found in the United States or Europe. In between these extremes, with modernization based primarily on income, most Jamaicans prepare their meals using a combination of old and new implements.

Visiting the island's plantation great houses one spots the time-honored elements of the Jamaican kitchen. Old-fashioned cooks still use the African **yabba**, an earthenware pot that's perfect for slow cooking, a **calabash**, which is a dried gourd used as a container, and the **kreng kreng**, a basket or wine container in which meat or fish can be smoked over an open fire. In some areas, huge wooden **mortars** are still used for pounding corn, plantain or yam, even though several more modern implements are also available.

To prepare authentic Jamaican food in kitchens around the world, requires little more than the standard equipment most people already have. In the preparatory phase of any island recipe, there are a few utensils that speed things along. The simple, inexpensive **mortar and pestle** comes in handy, if not for large jobs like pounding corn at least for small ones like grinding spices. A **blender**, **electric grinder** or **food processor** can also be used. Just be sure that you know the consistency of what you are trying to produce, then experiment until the finished product looks right. Younger cooks are also adopting the use of the **rice cooker**, which is quite a time saver.

The two most basic cooking vessels in the Jamaican kitchen are a heavy (traditionally cast-iron) **skillet** for the many dishes that require frying and a **large soup pot, kettle** or **Dutch oven** for those that need slow cooking.

For grilling or jerking meat, you will not need the misshapen and pock-marked 50-gallon oil drum that's most commonly used. **Gas grills** and **smokers** work just as well and do entirely acceptable jobs on Jamaican recipes that call for this cooking method.

Finally, for turning and lifting foods as they cook you can't do without a long-handled frying **spatula** and a **circular perforated ladle**. These come in different shapes and sizes, but you really need only one of each.

Like the slaves in the American South, the slaves and free Africans who formed the backbone of Jamaica's population faced mealtime with little prospect of quality, variety or freshness in their food. For quality and freshness they substituted the traditional cooking methods of the poor—frying, smothering and stewing—to make inexpensive meat savory.

For variety, however, they took spicing to a different level, borrowing first from the French and Spanish, then from the Indians and Chinese. The same dreary ingredients, these early Jamaicans learned, could be turned into lively meals with the creative use of spices.

Fried foods find particular favor in Jamaica. From Escoveitched Fish to the dozens of different fritters made with conch, saltfish or beans, crispy, well-seasoned foods are dear to the Jamaican heart. While health concerns about fried food are unlikely to go away, Jamaicans stress that eating them in moderation and frying them at the proper temperature to reduce oil absorption cuts fat and cholesterol considerably.

Second to frying as a cooking technique in the Jamaican kitchen is any variation on stewing. Whatever the island cook chooses to call his version, it's slow cooking that makes tough meat tender and bland food flavorful. The notion that a little bit of meat goes a long way to season vegetables is a basic premise of many delicious Jamaican dishes.

Surprisingly perhaps, there are many hot and hearty soups on the Jamaican menu that are prepared like every other slow-cooked dish, only with more water or stock. With the coming of professional chefs, the separate process of making stock has become part of Jamaican cuisine. Traditionally, though, the cook simply put all his or her ingredients into a big kettle, covered them with water and simmered them until they tasted terrific.

Other favored cooking methods include boiling, particularly of plantains and yams, and baking, especially of bananas and breadfruit. Grilling, of course, is common. Additional flavor is supplied to meats and vegetables alike by marinating, stuffing, and rubbing them with spices.

LEFT: The vibrant paintings in the dining room at Jake's Village give the place a festive atmosphere. The tables were painted by Jamaican artist Ritula Frankel. RIGHT: These cast-iron Dutch oven and covered skillet are basic utensils in Jamaican kitchens.

Authentic Jamaican Ingredients

Ackee is an ornamental tree from West Africa that bears a bright red fruit. When ripe it bursts open to reveal three large black seeds and a bright yellow flesh that is popular as a breakfast food throughout Jamaica. Ackee is poisonous if eaten before it is fully mature, and because of its toxicity, is subject to import restrictions and may be hard to obtain in some countries. Never open an ackee pod; it will open itself when it ceases to be toxic. Ackee is sold canned in West Indian markets.

Allspice berries are grown primarily in Jamaica. They are a whole spice tasting of nutmeg, cinnamon, black pepper and clove. Used in numerous Jamaican dishes such as Jerk Pork, ground allspice is sold in most supermarkets. Just to make things interesting, Jamaicans refer to allspice as "pimento."

Annatto is a reddish-yellow seed from a flowering tree native to the West

Indies and Central America. Islanders store their annatto seeds in oil—lending the oil a beautiful reddish color. Saffron, turmeric or red food coloring may be substituted.

Breadfruit is a large tree fruit with a pebbly green skin and potato-like flesh. It is edible when cooked and can be used in place of any starchy vegetable, rice or pasta. Breadfruit is picked before it ripens and is typically served baked, grilled, fried, boiled or roasted. It's even been known to turn up in preserves or in beverages. Substitute potato or sweet potato if unavailable.

Callaloo is what the Jamaicans call the large edible green leaves of the taro root, usually prepared as one would prepare turnip greens or collard greens. Spinach is a good substitute.

Cassava is a large root vegetable also known as tapioca, manioc or

yuca. It has a tough brown skin and very firm, nutritious white flesh. Ground cassava, used for cakes, is sold in packets in West Indian markets.

Cho-cho is a pear-shaped, light green squash with a mild flavor. It is known elsewhere as chayote. To prepare—peel, halve and remove the seed before slicing and cooking the flesh. Zucchini or summer squash make good substitutes.

Conch or sea snails, are a beloved part of Caribbean cuisine. Conch meat must be pounded or ground in a food processor, to make it tender. Substitute any firm, white fish.

Coconut is edible in both its young and mature forms. Both the water and the "jelly" of the green coconut find their way into island drinks, and meat from the mature coconut gives many desserts a Caribbean identity. Coconut cream and milk are now widely sold canned and in packets which are quick and convenient. They come in varying consistencies depending on the brand, and you will need to try them out and adjust the thickness by adding water as needed.

Goat meat is eaten with enthusiasm in only a few places in the world, and Jamaica is assuredly one of them. Some credit immigrants from India who searched in vain for mutton to prepare their beloved curry. Finding no lambs, they latched onto the next best thing—and curried goat became a Caribbean classic. Most first-timers find goat milder in flavor than lamb and an excellent substitute for lamb in most recipes. Of course, if you can't find goat, you can substitute lamb.

Guavas are small fruits with green or pink, seed-filled flesh. Guavas grow all over Jamaica and the fruit lends itself well to juices, jellies, preserves, fruit cups, sauces, cocktails and desserts. When green, guavas are slightly tart; when ripe, they are sweeter.

Kale, sometimes referred to as Chinese broccoli, is enjoyed for its firm texture and emphatic flavor. This leafy green vegetable is recognizable by the thick central stem and dull, thick leaves with a bluish tinge. Only the tender portions of the stems and young inner leaves are generally eaten as the outer leaves are quite bitter. The thicker stems are peeled and halved lengthwise before cooking. Substitute broccoli stems.

Nutmegs, Jamaican cooks insist, should be bought whole and grated only as needed. The spicy-sweet flavor of this aromatic fruit seed makes it an excellent addition to cakes, puddings and drinks.

Otaheiti apples are yet another fruit introduced from the Pacific by Captain Bligh—the pear-shaped otaheiti apple ranges from pink to ruby red in color and is usually eaten fresh, though it can be poached in red wine or turned into a refreshing cold drink. Substitute pears if unavailable.

Papaya, a native of South America, is still called by its Amerindian name of "pawpaw" by some Jamaicans. The papaya has an orange color when ripe, and its mild flavor resembles that of a summer squash, making it a nice complement to the sharper flavors of other fruits. Green papaya is often used as an ingredient in chutney or relishes and makes a nice main dish when stuffed. When ripe, it is eaten as a melon, or served in fruit salad. Papaya juice makes a refreshing drink when sweetened with condensed milk or sugar.

Pickapeppa sauce is a commercially bottled sauce that is a key ingredient in Jamaican cuisine. The sweet, sour and spicy mixture was developed by Jamaican Norman Nash in the early 1920s. It contains a combination of tomatoes, onions, cane vinegar, mango, raisins, tamarind, chilies, and secret spices that is aged in oak for one year. Pickapeppa is sold in well-stocked supermarkets and spice shops. If you cannot find it, use steak sauce instead.

Plantains, sometimes referred to as cooking bananas, are a starchy vegetable that look like bananas on steroids. A green (unripe) plantain will first turn yellow and then black if allowed to ripen at room temperature. As it ripens, the pulp becomes sweeter and less starchy, but never as a sweet as a banana. Plantains are increasingly found in well-stocked supermarkets. Substitute unripe bananas or sweet potatoes.

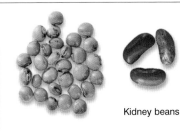

Kidney beans

Jamaicans refer to nearly all beans as peas. **Kidney beans** are the most popular. Fava beans and gungo peas, also known as pigeon peas, have been popular since their introduction to the island. **Gungo peas** are dried beans that have a sweet flavor. Light brown in color, they are especially popular in the West Indies, Africa and India. Gungo peas must be washed and soaked overnight in cold water and then cooked before using in soups and stews. Substitute black-eyed peas.

Saltfish refers to any dried, salted fish, most often cod. Saltfish is available in Italian, Spanish and Portuguese markets under the name *bacalao*.

Scotch bonnet chilies are the most popular chilies used in Jamaican cooking and are closely related to the Central American habañero chili. Ranging in color from yellow to orange to red, they are sold whole—both fresh and dried. Be sure to wear rubber gloves or wash your hands thoroughly after handling these chilies as the oils can burn the skin and eyes. You can substitute habañeros or bird's eye chilies, which have a similar heat, or jalapeños for a milder heat.

Sorrel, also known as roselle and flor de Jamaica, is a plant that produces deep red flowers that are dried and steeped in water to make a drink with a slightly tart taste and color similar to cranberry juice.

Soursop, notable for the spikes all over its green skin, has a perfumed flesh that's great in drinks or ice cream. Jamaicans believe soursop soothes the nerves—and the juice is often referred to as "nerve juice." The pulp is available frozen or canned.

Soy sauce was brought to Jamaica by Chinese laborers at the end of the nineteenth century. It is widely used in Jamaican cooking and adds a salty depth to many dishes. Black soy sauce is sweeter and less salty than regular soy and has caramel or molasses and wheat added to it.

Tamarind is a fragrant and tangy fruit that is used to flavor everything from drinks to curries to sauces—including Angostura bitters and Pickapeppa sauce. It is also an important ingredient in Jamaican folk medicine. Tamarind pulp or concentrate is sold in specialty Asian or Latin American food shops.

Taro, also known as cocoyam, dasheen and tannia, is a starchy tuber that is either served boiled as a vegetable, or is cut up and used as a thickener in hearty soups. While considered by some to have a texture and flavor superior to that of artichoke or potato, potatoes can often be used as a substitute in most recipes.

West Indian pumpkin, a member of the gourd, squash and melon family, is also known as *calabaza*. Possessing a sweet flavor similar to that of butternut squash, this firm-textured vegetable is used in soups, stews, breads and sweetened puddings. Though hardly the same, the best substitutes for *calabaza* are hubbard, butternut and acorn squash.

It's important never to confuse the tuberous yams in Jamaica with sweet potatoes. Cooked yams are more grainy and starchy then sweet potatoes, which tend to be soft and slightly sweet when cooked. The island's three favorite varieties of yams are white, yellow and yampee—all three are delicious either boiled or roasted.

Authentic Jamaican Recipes

Festival

1 cup (150 g) yellow cornmeal
³/₄ cup (100 g) flour
¹/₄ cup (60 g) packed light brown
 sugar
1 teaspoon baking powder
¹/₂ teaspoon salt
1 egg, lightly beaten
About 1 cup (250 ml) water
2 cups (500 ml) oil

1 Mix the dry ingredients in a medium-sized bowl. Stir the egg into the dry ingredients, adding enough water to make a soft dough. Tear off small handfuls of the dough and roll into ovals in your hands.
2 Heat the oil in heavy saucepan until very hot. Gently slide a few pieces of dough into the oil and deep-fry until golden brown, about 3 to 4 minutes. Remove and drain on paper towels.

Serves 4
Preparation time: 10 mins
Cooking time: 10 mins

Johnnycakes

2 cups (300 g) flour
1 tablespoon baking powder
¹/₂ teaspoon salt
1 teaspoon sugar
2 tablespoons vegetable shortening
About ¹/₂ cup (125 ml) water
Oil for deep-frying

1 In a medium bowl, sift together the flour, baking powder, salt and sugar. Add the shortening and, using your fingers or a pastry blender, combine until the mixture resembles coarse meal. Add enough water, a little at a time, to make a sticky dough.
2 Knead the dough on a floured surface until smooth, adding addi-tional flour if needed. Shape the dough into 2 in (5 cm) balls.
3 Heat the oil in a medium-sized frying pan until very hot. Deep-fry the Johnnycakes in batches until they are golden brown, about 2 to 3 minutes. Remove and drain on paper towels.

Serves 6 (2 Johnnycakes each)
Preparation time: 10 mins
Cooking time: 10 mins

Pie Crust

1 cup (150 g) flour
¹/₂ teaspoon salt
4 oz (125 g) plus 1 tablespoon butter
2–3 tablespoons cold water

1 Combine the flour and salt in a medium bowl. Add the butter and, using your fingers or a pastry blender, combine until the mixture resembles coarse meal. Add just enough water to make a smooth dough. Roll the dough into a ball, dust lightly with flour and cover with plastic wrap. Refrigerate for 30 minutes.
2 Roll out the dough on a lightly floured surface to an 11-in (28-cm) circle. Place in a 9-in (23-cm) pie dish and crimp the edge.

Note: To use as a prebaked crust, preheat the oven to 425°F (215°C). Fill the crust with 1 lb (500 g) of dried beans or pie weights sold in specialty shops. Bake until golden brown, about 15 minutes. Or, fill the unbaked crust with a desired filling and bake according to recipe directions.

Makes 1 crust
Preparation time: 45 mins

Beef Stock

1 lb (500 g) beef shanks, in pieces
3 lbs (1¹/₂ kg) beef soup bones
2 medium carrots, quartered
2 medium onions, quartered
3 stalks celery, coarsely chopped
2 leeks, white and light green parts
 only, coarsely chopped
2 cloves garlic
5 sprigs parsley
2 bay leaves
1 tablespoon black peppercorns
1 teaspoon salt
1 cup (250 ml) dry white wine
4 quarts (4 liters) water

1 In a large stockpot, combine all the ingredients and bring to a boil, skimming off the foam as it rises to the surface. Reduce the heat and simmer, partially covered, for 4 hours.
2 Remove all the solids and strain the stock through a sieve. Skim off as much fat as possible. Refrigerate or freeze to store.

Makes 2 quarts (2 liters)
Preparation time: 20 mins
Cooking time: 4 hours

Chicken Stock

1 chicken carcass
2 medium carrots, quartered
2 medium onions, quartered
3 stalks celery, coarsely chopped
2 leeks, coarsely chopped
2 cloves garlic
2 shallots, peeled and sliced
5 sprigs parsley
2 bay leaves
1 tablespoon black peppercorns
1 teaspoon salt
1 cup (250 ml) dry white wine
4 quarts (4 liters) water

1 In a large stockpot, combine all the ingredients and bring to a boil,

skimming off the foam as it rises to the surface. Reduce the heat and simmer, partially covered, for 4 hours.
2 Remove all the solids and strain the stock through a sieve. Skim off as much fat as possible.

Makes 2 quarts (2 liters)
Preparation time: 20 mins
Cooking time: 4 hours

Fish Stock

2 lbs (1 kg) fish bones, rinsed
2 medium onions, quartered
$^1/_2$ leeks, white and light green parts only, chopped
$^1/_2$ teaspoon dried thyme
1 bay leaf
1 teaspoon black peppercorns
1 cup (250 ml) dry white wine

1 In a large stockpot, combine all the ingredients, cover with water, and bring to a boil. Reduce the heat and simmer until the volume is reduced by half, about 1 hour. Skim the surface to remove any foam that rises to the surface.
2 Remove all the solids and strain the stock through a sieve. Skim the surface and set aside to cool.

Makes 1 quart (1 liter)
Preparation time: 10 mins
Cooking time: 1 hour

Curry Powder

You can buy premixed curry powders, but it's fun to make your own, and if you find a supply of fresh spices, the flavor is a lot richer too.

4 teaspoons ground coriander
4 teaspoons ground turmeric
4 teaspoons ground ginger
4 teaspoons ground black pepper
1 teaspoon ground cardamom
1 teaspoon ground cinnamon
1 teaspoon ground fenugreek

Mix all the ingredients together and store in an airtight jar.

Makes 6 tablespoons

Ackee and Saltfish

Considered the national dish of Jamaica, ackee and saltfish is popular as a hearty breakfast or as an appetizer at lunch or dinner.

1 lb (500 g) salted cod
2 dozen fresh ackee pods or 3 cups (12 oz/350 g) canned ackee
6 slices bacon, cut into small pieces
1 scotch bonnet or jalapeño chili, deseeded and sliced
2 spring onions, sliced
1 medium onion, diced
1 medium tomato, diced
$1/2$ teaspoon freshly ground black pepper

1 Soak the salted cod in cold water for 30 minutes, then drain and place in a pan with 4 cups (1 liter) of water. Bring to a boil, drain, then break the fish into flakes with a fork. Set aside.
2 If using fresh ackee, remove them from the pods. Discard the seeds and gently remove the pink membranes with a sharp knife. Parboil the pegs of ackee by covering them with salted water in a medium saucepan and bring just to a boil. Remove the saucepan from the heat, drain, and set aside.
3 Set a large skillet over medium heat and fry the bacon until crisp. Drain most of the fat from the skillet, reduce the heat to medium-low and add the chili, spring onions and onion, and sauté until tender. Add the salted cod, ackee, tomato and black pepper and cook over low heat for 5 minutes.
4 Use a slotted spoon to serve and accompany with boiled or pan-fried Plantain Chips (page 34) and Johnnycakes (page 26).

Serves 4   Preparation time: 45 mins   Cooking time: 15 mins

Table painted by Margaret Robson.

Stamp and Go

This favorite Jamaican snack is available at bus stops all over the island. Picture a rider jumping off the bus, buying and swallowing one of these treats, and then hopping back on the bus to continue his trip.

4 oz (125 g) salted codfish
6 tablespoons boiling water
1/2 cup (75 g) flour
3/4 teaspoon baking powder
1 medium onion, diced
1 clove garlic, minced
1 scotch bonnet or jalapeño chili,
   deseeded and minced
1 tablespoon thinly sliced chives
Salt and freshly ground pepper
1/2 teaspoon finely minced fresh
   thyme or a pinch of dried thyme
2 large eggs, separated
Oil for deep-frying
1 teaspoon tarragon or other herb-
   infused vinegar

Tomato Scotch Bonnet Sauce
5 large ripe tomatoes, blanched,
   peeled and quartered
1 large white onion, quartered
1–2 scotch bonnet or jalapeño chilies,
   deseeded
1 1/2 tablespoons brown sugar
2 teaspoons salt
1 cup (250 ml) malt vinegar

1 To make the Tomato Scotch Bonnet Sauce, purée the tomato, onion, and chili in a food processor. Transfer the purée to a saucepan and add the remaining ingredients. Cook the mixture over medium heat, stirring occasionally, until it begins to boil. Lower the heat and simmer for 20 minutes. Remove from the heat and set aside to cool.

2 Soak the codfish in water for a few hours or overnight. Drain and place the fish in a small bowl. Pour the boiling water over the fish and let it cool. Drain the codfish again, reserving the water. Rinse the fish in fresh cold water, remove any skin and bones, and break the fish into flakes with a fork. Set aside.

3 Place the flour and baking powder in a large bowl and gradually add the reserved water, stirring until thoroughly mixed. Add the fish, onion, garlic, chili, chives, salt, pepper, thyme and egg yolks to the flour mixture, stirring until combined.

4 Heat the oil in a deep skillet over medium-high heat. Beat the egg whites until stiff and fold them into the fish mixture along with the vinegar. Drop the batter by tablespoons into the hot oil and fry until golden brown. Remove from the skillet with a slotted spoon and drain on paper towels. Serve hot with the Tomato Scotch Bonnet Sauce.

Serves 6   Preparation time: 30 mins + overnight for soaking the codfish
Cooking time: 35 mins

Table painted by Margaret Robson.

Seafood Fritters

Sweet mango salsa complements the salty flavors of plantain chips and conch or codfish fritters.

8 oz (250 g) conch or salted codfish, soaked and drained
1/2 green bell pepper, deseeded and diced
1/2 stalk celery, diced
1/2 small onion, diced
1 tablespoon tomato paste
1 tablespoon lemon juice
Pinch of cayenne pepper
1 cup (150 g) flour
1/2 teaspoon baking powder
1/2 cup (125 ml) cold water
Oil for deep-frying
Cocktail sauce or Mango Salsa (recipe below)

1 If using conch, rinse and pat it dry. Process the conch or salted codfish in a food processor until finely ground. Transfer to a bowl and add the bell pepper, celery, onion, tomato paste, lemon juice and cayenne pepper. Mix thoroughly and let it stand for 10 minutes. Then stir in the flour, baking powder and enough water to make a thick batter.
2 Heat the oil in a deep saucepan over medium-high heat until a drop of batter sizzles and moves around the pan. Drop tablespoon-size portions of batter in the oil, one or two at a time, and fry until golden brown on all sides. Remove from the saucepan with a slotted spoon and drain on paper towels. Repeat with the remaining batter.
3 Serve hot with cocktail sauce or Mango Salsa for dipping.

Serves 6   Preparation time: 20 mins   Cooking time: 15 mins

Plantain Chips

4 green plantains or large green bananas
2 cups (500 ml) oil
Salt, to taste

1 Peel the plantains or bananas and slice them diagonally or lengthwise into 1/4-in (6-mm) thin pieces.
2 Heat the oil in a large, deep skillet over medium-high heat and fry half the chips until golden brown, about 5 minutes. Remove the chips from the pan with a slotted spoon and drain on paper towels. Dust lightly with salt. Repeat with the remainder of the chips.

Serves 6   Preparation time: 5 mins   Cooking time: 10 mins

Mango Salsa

2 large ripe mangoes, peeled, pitted and diced
1/4 cup (40 g) minced red onion
1 scotch bonnet chili, deseeded and minced
2 tablespoons fresh lime juice
1 tablespoon minced fresh coriander leaves (cilantro)
1/4 teaspoon salt

Combine all the ingredients in a bowl and mix thoroughly. Refrigerate for 1 hour before serving.

Makes 2 cups (500 ml)   Preparation time: 10 mins

Carved wood platter and
ceramic bowl from Patoo Gallery.

Steamed Callaloo Pastries with Ackee Sauce

This recipe from Everett Wilkerson of the Grand Lido Sans Souci is a good example of what young chefs in Jamaica are doing today—combining the New World ingredients callaloo and ackee in a way that is reminiscent of Greek *spanakopita*.

1 tablespoon butter
1 clove garlic, minced
1 small onion, minced
$1/2$ scotch bonnet or jalapeño chili, deseeded and minced
$1/4$ teaspoon fresh thyme or a pinch of dried thyme
2 lbs (1 kg) callaloo leaves, or fresh spinach, washed and dried,
  tough stems discarded
1 medium tomato, diced
Salt and freshly ground black pepper, to taste
$2^1/_2$ cups (10 oz/300 g) shredded cheddar cheese
8 sheets phyllo dough
Oil for brushing

Ackee Sauce
1 bay leaf
10 white peppercorns
4 oz (125 ml) white wine
5 cups ($1^1/_4$ liters) heavy cream
12 oz (350 g) cooked fresh or canned ackee, squeezed of all water, and puréed
8 oz (250 g) butter, cut into tablespoons
Salt and freshly ground pepper, to taste

1 Melt the butter in a large skillet over medium heat. Add the garlic, onion, chili and thyme, and sauté until the onion is tender. Stir in the callaloo and tomato, and cook for 5 to 7 minutes. Season with salt and black pepper, and set aside to cool. Stir in the cheese.
2 On a clean, dry surface, lay out the phyllo, one sheet at a time. Brush each sheet lightly with oil and place $1/_8$ of the callaloo mixture along the edge of one sheet. Roll up the edge to cover the filling and then fold in the ends. Roll up the sheet and brush the top with a bit more oil. Repeat with the remaining phyllo sheets and filling.
3 To make the Ackee Sauce, place the bay leaf and peppercorns in a saucepan, cover with the wine, and bring to a boil. Reduce the heat to medium-low and cook until most of the liquid is gone, about 3 to 5 minutes. Strain the reduced liquid and return it to the saucepan. Add the heavy cream and simmer until the liquid is reduced to approximately 2 cups (500 ml), about 5 to 7 minutes. Add the puréed ackee and simmer for 1 minute. Remove from the heat and whisk in the butter, one tablespoon at a time. Season with salt and pepper.
4 Preheat the oven to 350°F (175°C). Place the phyllo rolls, seam side down, on a baking sheet and bake until golden brown, about 10 minutes. Serve hot with the Ackee Sauce.

Makes 8 rolls   Preparation time: 20 mins   Cooking time: 40 mins

Red Pea Soup with Spinners

A traditional hearty Jamaican stew, recipe from Nigel Clarke and Clifton Wright at the Grand Lido Negril, is scented with fresh thyme and topped with thin dumplings called Spinners.

1½ lbs (700 g) stewing beef, cubed
12 oz (350 g) ham, diced
2 cups (400 g) dried kidney beans
  soaked overnight and drained
4 quarts (4 liters) water
2 scotch bonnet or jalapeño chilies
3 medium potatoes or yams, peeled
  and cubed
3 spring onions
1 sprig of fresh thyme or ½ teaspoon
  dried thyme
Pinch of salt

Spinners
1 cup (150 g) flour
Pinch of salt
⅓ cup (90 ml) water

1 Place the beef, ham, kidney beans, and water in a large stockpot over medium-high heat. Bring to a boil, reduce the heat to low and simmer, covered, about 2 hours until the beans are soft.
2 To make the Spinners, combine the flour and salt in a small bowl. Add enough water to make a stiff dough. Pinch off about 2 tablespoons of the dough and shape into long, thin pieces. Set aside.
3 Add the whole chilies, potatoes or yams, spring onions and thyme to the stockpot, and simmer for 15 minutes. Add the Spinners and simmer for another 15 minutes until the potatoes are almost tender.

Serves 6   Preparation time: 20 mins   Cooking time: 2½ hours

Coco Breads

2 tablespoons yeast
1 teaspoon sugar
¼ cup (60 ml) warm water
¾ cup (185 ml) warm milk
1½ teaspoons salt
1 egg, lightly beaten
3 cups (450 g) flour
4 oz (125 g) butter, melted

1 In a large bowl, dissolve the yeast and the sugar in the water. Stir in the milk, salt and egg. Add half the flour and mix well, continuing to add flour until the dough forms a ball. Turn the dough out onto a dry, lightly floured surface and knead for 10 minutes until smooth but firm.
2 Oil a clean bowl and turn the dough in it until coated. Cover with a damp towel and set aside to rise for 1 hour. Cut the dough into 10 portions. Roll each portion into a 6-in (15-cm) circle, brush with a little butter, then fold in half. Brush with more butter and fold in half again. Set the breads on a greased baking sheet and let them rise until they double in bulk, about 20 minutes.
3 Preheat the oven to 425°F (220°C) and set a pan of hot water on the lowest oven rack. Bake the breads for 12 to 15 minutes until golden.

Makes 10 large rolls   Preparation time: 2 hours   Cooking time: 15 mins

Plates and bowl from The Craft Cottage;
napkin from Patoo Gallery.

Pepperpot

The Caribbean's most famous soup—a peppery concoction made rich and thick with okra. This version is from the Terra Nova in Kingston.

2 lbs (1 kg) fresh kale washed and dried, tough stems discarded
8 oz (250 g) callaloo or fresh spinach, washed and dried, tough
  stems discarded
20 pods fresh okra
4 oz (125 g) salt pork, cut into thin strips
8 oz (250 g) lean pork, cubed
2 medium onions, thinly sliced
2 scotch bonnet or jalapeño chilies, deseeded and sliced
1 tablespoon chopped fresh thyme or 1 teaspoon dried thyme
1 teaspoon ground cumin
Pinch of freshly ground black pepper
6 cups (1$^1/_2$ liters) chicken stock
4 oz (125 g) medium shrimp, in their shells (optional)

1 Roughly chop the kale and callaloo or spinach and set aside. Dice the okra and set aside.
2 Heat a stockpot over medium heat and sauté the salt pork for 10 minutes. Discard all but 2 tablespoons of the rendered fat, add the pork and onions, and sauté until the onions are translucent, about 5 minutes.
3 Add the kale, callaloo, and the remaining ingredients except the shrimp. Cover and simmer for 2 hours. About 5 minutes before serving, add the shrimp, if using, and cook until they turn pink. Discard the salt pork and serve.

Note: If using spinach instead of callaloo, it should be added to the pot after the soup has simmered for 1$^1/_2$ hours.

Serves 6–8   Preparation time: 15 mins   Cooking time: 2 hours 15 mins

Soup bowl and carved chickens from Patoo Gallery;
painted screen and clothesline by Inga Girvan Hunter.

Gungo Pea Soup

A traditional soup that had been confined to the Christmas and New Year's holiday season, Gungo Pea Soup is now enjoyed throughout the year. This version is from Winsome Warren at Jake's Village. Also known as congo or pigeon peas, gungo peas are of West African origin.

2 cups (400 g) dried gungo or
   pigeon peas
1 smoked ham hock
2 medium onions, cut into large pieces
2 carrots, cut into large pieces
1 stalk celery, with leaves
2 scotch bonnet or jalapeño chilies,
   deseeded and diced
1 clove garlic, minced
1 bay leaf
$1/_2$ teaspoon crushed fresh rosemary
   leaves or $1/_4$ teaspoon crushed
   dried rosemary
8 oz (250 g) smoked sausage, sliced
1 portion Spinners (page 38)

1 Prepare the Spinners by following the instructions on page 38.
2 Wash the peas and place them in a bowl. Add enough water to cover and soak overnight. Drain and set aside.
3 Add 6 cups ($1^1/_2$ liters) of water to a stockpot and add the ham hock, onions, carrots, celery, chilies, garlic, bay leaf and rosemary. Bring to a boil, reduce the heat to low and simmer for 45 minutes. Strain the stock, reserving the ham hock and discarding the vegetables. Skim the fat from the stock.
4 Return the stock and the ham hock to the stockpot along with the soaked peas. Simmer over low heat until the peas are tender, about 2 hours. Remove half of the peas from the soup with a slotted spoon and purée in a food processor. Return the purée to the soup. Add the smoked sausage slices and prepared Spinners to the soup and heat through.

Serves 6–8   Preparation time: 10 mins   Cooking time: 2 hours 45 mins

Curry Pumpkin

A tasty vegetarian stew that is traditionally made with green-skinned West Indian pumpkin, which is similar in texture and flavor to sugar pumpkin or butternut squash.

2 tablespoons oil
1 medium onion, diced
2 tablespoons curry powder
1 green bell pepper, deseeded and
   sliced
2 lbs (1 kg) peeled and cubed pumpkin or butternut squash
2 cups (500 ml) water
1 cup (250 ml) coconut milk
1 scotch bonnet or jalapeño chili,
   sliced (optional)
2 cups (130 g) cooked gungo or
   pigeon peas

1 Heat the oil in large skillet over medium heat. Add the onion and sauté until translucent, about 5 minutes. Add the curry powder and sauté for a few seconds, until fragrant.
2 Add the green bell pepper and pumpkin or butternut squash and mix well. Add the water, coconut milk and chili, and simmer over low heat for 45 minutes until the pumpkin is tender.
3 Stir in the gungo peas and serve over rice.

Note: To save time preparing this recipe, purchase cubed fresh or frozen butternut squash.

Serves 4   Preparation time: 30 mins   Cooking time: 50 mins

Table painted by Ritula Frankel.

Pumpkin Soup

Jamaica's love affair with the pumpkin is consummated in this soup which is spiked with fresh ginger—another flavor that islanders can't seem to get enough of. This delicious version is from the Terra Nova in Kingston.

2 lbs (1 kg) beef, cubed
4 quarts (4 liters) water
2 lbs (1 kg) pumpkin or butternut
   squash, peeled and cubed
1 lb (500 g) yams, peeled and cubed
1 clove garlic
1 sprig fresh thyme or $1/2$ teaspoon
   dried thyme
Salt and freshly ground black pepper
1 tablespoon freshly grated ginger

1 Place the beef in a large soup pot, cover with the water, and bring to a boil. Reduce the heat to low and simmer, uncovered, until the beef is tender, about $1^1/_2$ hours. Add the pumpkin, yams, garlic and thyme, and continue to cook until the pumpkin and yams are tender, about 45 minutes.
2 Remove the pumpkin and yam from the stock with a slotted spoon and purée in a food processor. Return the vegetable purée to the stock. Alternatively, use an immersion blender to purée the soup.
3 Season the soup with salt and pepper. Sprinkle each serving with the grated ginger and serve.

Serves 8–10   Preparation time: 20 mins   Cooking time: 2 hours 15 mins

Bammie

This fried bread, also from the Terra Nova, is made with ground cassava, which is available in West Indian and Hispanic markets.

Oil, for greasing
$1^1/_2$ lbs (750 g) cassava root
   or 3 cups ground cassava
$1/_2$ teaspoon salt
4 cups (1 liter) water

1 If using cassava root, peel and grate the cassava to make 3 cups of grated cassava. Place it in a cloth and wring out as much liquid as possible. Then mix the grated cassava or ground cassava and salt in a large bowl and slowly stir in enough water to form dough. Divide the dough into 6 equal pieces.
2 Grease a skillet with a little oil. Place 1 piece of dough in the greased skillet and press down until the bammie is about 6 in (15 cm) in diameter (Jamaicans often use the bottom of a floured bottle for this task). Place the skillet over medium heat.
3 When steam starts to rise and the Bammie's edge shrinks slightly from the edge of the skillet (after about 5 minutes), press it flat again and turn it over. Cook for another 5 minutes. Repeat with the remaining pieces of dough, greasing the skillet as necessary.

Serves 6   Preparation time: 15 mins   Cooking time: 1 hour

Calabash balls painted by Jasmine Thomas-Girvan.

Oxtail and Beans

The combination of fava beans, oxtail stew and Spinners gives this recipe from Norma Shirley of Norma at the Wharfhouse that extraordinary country flavor that the best Jamaican dishes possess.

2 lbs (1 kg) oxtail or beef or veal shanks
4 tablespoons oil
5 cups (1$^1/_4$ liters) water
2 medium tomatoes, diced
2 medium onions, diced
1 sprig fresh thyme or $^1/_2$ teaspoon dried thyme
Salt and freshly ground black pepper, to taste
8 oz (250 g) cooked fresh or canned fava beans
1 portion Spinners (page 38)

1 Prepare the Spinners by following the instructions on page 38.
2 Wash and dry the oxtail and cut it into serving pieces at the joints. If using beef or veal shanks, cut them into serving pieces (you can ask your butcher to do this). Brown the meat in the oil in a large stockpot over medium-high heat. Add 4 cups (1 liter) of the water and bring to a boil over high heat. Reduce the heat to low and simmer until the meat is tender, about 1 hour.
3 Add the remaining ingredients, except the remaining water, beans and Spinners, and cook over medium heat for 10 minutes. Add the remaining 1 cup (250 ml) of water along with the beans and the Spinners. Reduce the heat to low, cover and simmer until the liquid becomes a thick gravy, about 10 minutes.

Serves 4   Preparation time: 25 mins   Cooking time: 1$^1/_2$ hours

Painted calabash candleholder, birdhouse, maracas, and table mat from The Craft Cottage.

Run Down

This dish wears its heritage both in its name and in its ingredients. It is quick and made with the tropical flavors closest at hand. The photograph shows the dish served with breadfruit, but you can also serve it with plantains.

3 tablespoons freshly squeezed
   lime juice
2 lbs (1 kg) mackerel or other oily
   fish fillets
3 cups (750 ml) coconut milk
1 large onion, diced
2 cloves garlic, sliced
1 scotch bonnet or jalapeño chili,
   deseeded and minced
1 lb (500 g) ripe tomatoes, blanched,
   peeled and diced
1 tablespoon cider vinegar
1 teaspoon dried thyme
Salt and freshly ground black pepper

1 Pour the lime juice over the fish fillets in a shallow bowl and set aside.
2 In a large, heavy skillet cook the coconut milk until it turns oily about 5 to 7 minutes. Add the onion, garlic and chili, and cook until tender, about 5 minutes. Stir in the tomatoes, vinegar, thyme, and salt and pepper. Add the fish, cover, and cook until the fish flakes easily when tested with a fork, about 10 minutes.

Serves 6   Preparation time: 15 mins   Cooking time: 25 mins

Baked Plantains

Unripe plantains, baked in their skins like potatoes, make a satisfying side dish.

4 green plantains, unpeeled

1 Preheat the oven to 375°F (190°C). Line a baking sheet with aluminum foil.
2 Wash and dry the plantains and trim off the tips. Cut a lengthwise slit in each fruit and set them, slit-side up on the prepared baking sheet. Bake for 40 minutes in the preheated oven until tender.
3 When cool enough to handle, peel the plantains and slice them into lengthwise strips or crosswise in rounds. Serve warm.

Serves 4–6   Preparation time: 5 mins   Cooking time: 40 mins

Baked Breadfruit

8 oz (250 g) butter
1 teaspoon ground cinnamon
1/2 teaspoon freshly grated nutmeg
   or ground nutmeg
1 ripe breadfruit
1/2 cup (100 g) brown sugar

1 Preheat the oven to 350°F (175°C). Melt the butter and mix in the cinnamon and nutmeg. Set aside.
2 Remove the stem and scoop out the inside of the breadfruit. Cut it into quarters and then into thick wedges. Arrange the wedges on a baking sheet lined with foil and drizzle with the spiced butter.
3 Bake for 15 minutes, then turn the wedges over and bake an additional 10 to 15 minutes until the wedges are tender. Sprinkle with the brown sugar and serve warm.

Serves 4   Preparation time: 15 mins   Cooking time: 25 mins

Parrot tray from Magic Kitchen.

Scotch Bonnet Grilled Fish

Jamaica's beloved chili—the scotch bonnet—gives this grilled fish extra kick. Festival (recipe on page 26), shown as an accompaniment in the photograph at right, complements this recipe from Martin Maginley of the Grand Lido Negril nicely.

1 teaspoon dried tarragon
1 teaspoon dried basil
1 teaspoon dried thyme
1 teaspoon dried oregano
1 teaspoon paprika
1 teaspoon fennel seed
1 teaspoon aniseed
2 cups (500 ml) oil
2 tablespoons freshly squeezed lemon juice
2 tablespoons freshly squeezed lime juice
2 tablespoons Worcestershire sauce
1 tablespoon white wine
1 scotch bonnet or jalapeño chili, deseeded and minced
6 small, whole white fish (like snapper), or 3 lbs (1½ kg) fish fillets

1 Preheat the grill. In a shallow bowl, combine all of the ingredients except the fish and mix well. Coat each fish or fillet in the spice mix, turning to cover evenly.
2 Grill the fish over medium heat, turning once, until it flakes easily when tested with a fork, about 15 minutes.

Serves 6   Preparation time: 5 mins   Cooking time: 15 mins

Pepper Shrimp

Bandannaed Jamaican ladies sell these bright orange treats in little plastic bags on the side of the road.

1 cup (250 ml) oil
2 scotch bonnet or jalapeño chilies, deseeded and minced
2 cloves garlic, minced
2 teaspoons salt
5 lbs (2½ kg) shrimp, in the shell
2 tablespoons cider vinegar

Heat the oil, chilies, garlic and salt in a heavy Dutch oven or stockpot over medium-high heat. Add the shrimp and cook, stirring frequently, for 3 minutes. Sprinkle the shrimp with the vinegar and cook, stirring frequently for another 3 minutes until the shrimp turn pink.

Serves 6–8   Preparation time: 5 mins   Cooking time: 8 mins

Bowl from The Craft Cottage.

Smoked Marlin Salad

Here's a delicious creation from James Palmer of Strawberry Hill. Smoked marlin is eaten around Port Antonio, especially during the legendary autumn marlin tournament. At that time, this sleepy north coast town is transformed into a reggae version of Hemingway's Pamplona. The marlin that isn't immediately devoured as steaks is carried off to the smoker, where it takes on a milder salmon-like flavor and texture that holds up well when thinly sliced.

1 lb (500 g) smoked marlin or salmon or other smoked fish, thinly sliced
1 lb (500 g) mixed salad greens

Mango Chutney
1 large ripe mango, peeled and pitted
1 scotch bonnet or jalapeño chili
1 cup (250 ml) white wine

Pickled Onion
2 large onions, thinly sliced
2 cups (500 ml) cider vinegar
$1/_8$ teaspoon each allspice, cumin and thyme
1 bay leaf
1 tablespoon sugar

Guacamole
2 large ripe avocados, peeled and pitted
Juice of 1 lime
1 small tomato, deseeded and diced
1 small onion, minced
$1/_2$ scotch bonnet or jalapeño chili, deseeded and minced

1 To prepare the Mango Chutney, combine the mango, chili and white wine in a small saucepan and cook over medium-high heat until soft, about 20 minutes. Remove from the heat and set aside to cool.
2 To prepare the Pickled Onion, combine all the ingredients in a medium saucepan and cook over medium-high heat for 30 minutes. Remove from the heat and set aside to cool.
3 Prepare the Guacamole by mashing the avocado. Add the remaining ingredients, mix well and set aside.
4 To assemble the salad, place a small amount of the salad greens on each of 4 dinner plates, then drape some of the sliced marlin over the salad. Serve with the three condiments.

Serves 4   Preparation time: 20 mins   Cooking time: 30 mins

Hand-painted ceramic plate and bowl by Margaret McGhie.

Brown Gravy Fish

A simple, old-fashioned braised fish deliciously put together by Thomas Swan of the Grand Lido Negril. It is served with a well-seasoned corn bread or polenta.

2 lbs (1 kg) mild white fish fillets
1 cup (150 g) flour
2 tablespoons oil
2 medium onions, diced
3 carrots, peeled and diced
8 oz (250 g) green beans, cut into thirds
2 spring onions, sliced
2 ripe tomatoes, diced
1 quart (1 liter) fish stock or water

1 Dredge the fish fillets in the flour. Heat the oil in a large skillet over medium-high heat and fry the fish until golden brown on both sides, about 5 to 8 minutes. Remove the fish and set aside to drain on paper towels.
2 Drain most of the oil from the skillet and add the onions, carrots, green beans, and spring onions. Sauté until the vegetables are tender-crisp, about 5 minutes. Add the tomatoes and fish stock, and simmer for 8 minutes.
3 Return the fish to the skillet, cover, and simmer until heated through, about 10 minutes. Serve hot with Turn Polenta.

Serves 6   Preparation time: 20 mins   Cooking time: 20 mins

Turn Polenta

4 tablespoons oil
1 large ripe tomato, diced
1 large green bell pepper, deseeded
  and diced
12 okra pods, sliced
1 large onion, diced
1 spring onion, sliced
1 clove garlic, minced
Salt and freshly ground black pepper
1 quart (1 liter) water
2 cups (300 g) polenta or yellow
  cornmeal

1 Heat the oil in a large skillet over medium-high heat. Add all the vegetables and sauté until tender, about 8 minutes. Add the salt, pepper and water, and bring to a boil.
2 Gradually stir in the polenta or cornmeal and reduce the heat to medium. Stir vigorously until thick, about 10 minutes. Once the mixture is smooth, cover and cook in the skillet over low heat for 30 minutes. Remove the skillet from the heat and let the polenta cool slightly.
3 Turn the polenta onto a large serving plate and cut into wedges. To make rounds (as in the photo opposite), form the mixture into patties.

Serves 6   Preparation time: 10 mins   Cooking time: 50 mins

Steamed Fish and Tea

This delicious fish recipe from Mark Cole of the Grand Lido Sans Souci uses fresh vegetables simmered in fish stock to make a delicate but flavorful brew for this light and healthy dish. In Jamaica, any broth is called tea. Here a flavorful fish broth is used to accompany the fish.

2 cups (500 ml) fish stock
2 carrots, peeled and diced
1 onion, diced
8–10 okra pods, sliced
2 cho-chos (chayote), or 1 medium zucchini or summer squash, diced
2 medium potatoes, peeled and diced
1$^1/_2$ cups (350 g) diced pumpkin or 1 medium sweet potato, peeled and diced
2 sprigs fresh thyme leaves or 1 teaspoon dried thyme
1–2 scotch bonnet or jalapeño chilies, deseeded and minced
1 spring onion, sliced
1 clove garlic, minced
Salt and freshly ground black pepper
1$^1/_2$ lbs (700 g) white fish fillets

Fish Seasoning
1 ripe tomato, deseeded and diced
1 spring onion, thinly sliced
1 sprig fresh thyme or $^1/_2$ teaspoon dried thyme
1 clove garlic, minced
1 scotch bonnet or jalapeño chili, minced
$^1/_4$ cup (60 ml) fresh lime juice
Salt and freshly ground black pepper

1 Place the fish stock, carrots, onion, okra, cho-chos, potatoes, pumpkin, thyme, chilies, spring onions and garlic in a stockpot and simmer for 10 minutes until the vegetables are tender. Remove half the vegetables from the tea with a slotted spoon and set aside. Season the tea with salt and pepper.
2 To make the Fish Seasoning, combine all of the ingredients in a shallow dish. Dredge the fish fillets in it to coat them on all sides. Place the fillets on a clean, dry work surface. Distribute the reserved vegetable mixture among the fillets, roll up the fillets and secure them with toothpicks.
3 Steam the fillets until the fish flakes easily when tested with a fork, about 10 minutes. Remove the fish from the steamer and keep warm. Slice the fillets into rounds and serve with the fish tea and vegetables.

Serves 4–6   Preparation time: 20 mins   Cooking time: 25 minutes

Roasted Red Snapper with Vegetables

A quick and savory dish that needs only a side of rice for a complete meal. Both recipes are from Winsome Warren of Jake's Village

2 lbs (1 kg) whole snappers, cleaned and scaled or 1¹/₂ lbs (700 g) snapper fillets
¹/₂ cup (125 ml) fresh lime juice
Salt and freshly ground black pepper
¹/₂ cup (125 ml) olive oil
1 large onion, thinly sliced
1 teaspoon fresh thyme
   or ¹/₂ teaspoon dried thyme
¹/₂ teaspoon fresh oregano
1 bay leaf, crumbled
1 medium onion, diced
3 carrots, peeled and sliced
8 oz (250 g) callaloo or spinach, washed, tough stems discarded
2 cloves garlic, minced
1 scotch bonnet or jalapeño chili, deseeded and minced
1 tablespoon chopped fresh parsley

1 Rub the fish inside and out with the lime juice, then season with salt and pepper, and set aside to marinate. Pour 6 tablespoons of the olive oil into a large roasting pan or baking dish. Arrange the onion slices on the bottom of the pan and sprinkle them with thyme, oregano and bay leaf. Sprinkle with additional salt and pepper.
2 Drain the fish, reserving the lime juice; pour the reserved lime juice over the onions in the pan. Place the snapper on top of the onions.
3 Preheat the oven to 400°F (200°C). Heat the remaining 2 tablespoons of olive oil in a skillet over medium heat and sauté all of the remaining ingredients for 3 minutes. Place the sautéed vegetables around the fish and bake, uncovered, until the fish flakes easily when tested with a fork, about 20 to 30 minutes.

Note: This dish can also be cooked over a grill. Place the onions, fish and sautéed vegetables on aluminum foil and wrap to make a pouch. Place the aluminum foil packets on a medium-hot grill for about 20 minutes.

Serves 6   Preparation time: 20 mins   Cooking time: 35 mins

Spanish Town Scotch Bonnet Shrimp

Sweet and tangy, this pepper and shrimp dish is made as spicy or as mild as you like by the addition of Jamaica's favorite chili—the scotch bonnet.

2 oz (60 g) unsalted butter
1 large onion, diced
1 green bell pepper, deseeded and thinly sliced
1–2 scotch bonnet or jalapeño chilies, deseeded and minced
1 clove garlic, minced
4 ripe tomatoes, diced
1 tablespoon fresh lime juice
1 bay leaf
1 teaspoon minced fresh parsley
¹/₂ teaspoon sugar
Salt and freshly ground black pepper
1 teaspoon Worcestershire sauce
1 teaspoon Pickapeppa sauce or steak sauce
1¹/₂ lbs (700 g) medium shrimp, peeled and deveined

1 Melt the butter in a large skillet over medium heat and add the onion, bell pepper, chilies and garlic, and sauté until the vegetables are tender but not browned, about 5 minutes.
2 Add the tomato, lime juice, bay leaf, parsley and sugar. Season with salt and pepper, and mix well. Simmer, uncovered, until the sauce is slightly reduced, about 5 minutes.
3 Remove the bay leaf and stir in the Worcestershire sauce and Pickapeppa sauce. Add the shrimp and cook until they turn pink, about 3 minutes. Serve with rice.

Serves 6   Preparation time: 20 mins   Cooking time: 15 mins

Fried Fish with Coconut

Beer, grated coconut and callaloo make these dishes from the Terra Nova restaurant a quintessential island dish.

1$^1/_2$ lbs (700 g) snapper or other white fish fillets
Salt and freshly ground black pepper
2 eggs
1$^3/_4$ cups (250 g) flour
$^3/_4$ cup (185 ml) beer
1 tablespoon baking powder
3 cups (450 g) grated fresh or 2$^1/_4$ cups (180 g) unsweetened dried coconut
4 tablespoons oil

1 Season the fish fillets with salt and pepper.
2 In a bowl, combine the eggs, 1$^1/_4$ cups (185 g) of the flour, beer and baking powder and mix well to make a smooth batter. Place the remaining $^1/_2$ cup (75 g) of the flour in a shallow dish and place the coconut in another shallow dish.
3 Heat the oil in a large skillet over medium-high heat. Dredge the fish fillets in the flour, shaking off any excess, then dip in the beer batter. Coat generously with the grated coconut and place in the skillet. Repeat with the remaining fillets. Pan-fry the fish until golden brown, turning once, about 3 to 5 minutes per side. Remove from the skillet and drain on paper towels. Serve with freshly sliced carrots on the side.

Serves 6   Preparation time: 15 mins   Cooking time: 10 mins

Sautéed Callaloo

2 lbs (1 kg) callaloo or spinach, washed and dried, tough stems discarded
4 oz (125 g) butter
1 scotch bonnet or jalapeño chili, sliced
Salt and freshly ground black pepper

Roughly chop the callaloo or spinach. Heat the butter in a large skillet over medium heat. Add the callaloo or spinach and chili, and season with salt and pepper. Sauté until just wilted, about 3 minutes.

Serves 6   Preparation time: 5 mins   Cooking time: 5 mins

Hand-painted ceramics plate and bowl by Margaret McGhie; woodcarving and table from Living Wood.

Braised Blue Mountain Lamb

A delightful dish from James Palmer at the Strawberry Hill restaurant with a host of hot, bitter and sweet flavors from the island repertoire.

6 lamb shanks, trimmed
Salt and freshly ground black pepper
4 tablespoons butter
Zest of 2 oranges, grated
2 cups (500 ml) freshly squeezed orange juice
1 tablespoon cider vinegar
1 bay leaf
$1/2$ teaspoon angostura bitters
$1/2$ teaspoon Pickapeppa sauce or steak sauce
$1/2$ cup (125 ml) chicken stock

1 Season the lamb shanks with salt and pepper. Melt the butter in a Dutch oven or large skillet over medium-high heat. Add the lamb and cook until browned on all sides, about 10 minutes. Reduce the heat to low, add the remaining ingredients, and cook until the lamb is tender, about $1^{1}/_{2}$ hours.
2 Transfer the lamb shanks to a serving dish and cover to keep warm. Skim and discard the excess fat from the pan liquid. Bring the remaining liquid to a boil over high heat, reduce the heat to medium, and simmer for 10 minutes (the liquid will reduce). Add the chicken stock to adjust the consistency and flavor of the sauce.
3 Pour the sauce over the lamb shanks and serve with mashed potatoes, fried onions, and Sautéed Callaloo (page 60).

Serves 6   Preparation time: 5 mins   Cooking time: 2 hours

Plate underlay from Strawberry Hill Gift shop.

Curried Goat or Lamb

Jamaicans can thank Indian immigrants for bringing this addictive curry dish to the island. This delicious version is from Sydney Wilson of the Grand Lido Negril.

2 tablespoons oil
$1^1/_2$ lbs (700 g) goat or lamb, cut into small cubes
3 large onions, diced
2 cloves garlic, minced
2 tablespoons curry powder
2 large potatoes, diced
2 ripe tomatoes, diced
3 cups (750 ml) chicken stock
1 tablespoon wine vinegar
$^1/_2$ teaspoon salt
1 teaspoon paprika
1 bay leaf

1 Heat the oil in a large pot or Dutch oven over medium heat, and brown the meat in batches. Remove the meat with a slotted spoon and set aside. Sauté the onions and garlic in the drippings until soft but not brown, about 5 minutes.
2 Stir in the curry powder and potatoes, and cook for about 3 minutes to release the curry flavor.
3 Add the tomato, stock, vinegar, salt and paprika. Return the meat to the pan, cover and simmer for $1^1/_2$ hours. Add $^1/_2$ cup (125 ml) water if the mixture becomes too dry. Add the bay leaf and cook for 30 minutes more until the meat is tender. Remove the bay leaf and serve with plain rice or Rice and Peas (page 77).

Serves 4   Preparation time: 20 mins   Cooking time: 2 hours 10 mins

Photo at left shows Curried Goat (bottom) served with Rice and Peas (top right—recipe given on page 77) and Mannish Water (top left; recipe not given). Wooden bowls and tray from The Craft Cottage.

Beef Tenderloin with Ackee and Vegetables

This delicious recipe of beef tenderloin paired with rustic island ackee and callaloo is from Martin Maginley of the Grand Lido Negril and is served stacked high for a dramatic presentation.

4 tablespoons olive oil
1 small onion, diced
1 head garlic, minced
2 cups (500 ml) dry red wine
3 cups (750 ml) beef stock
Salt and freshly ground black pepper
2 tablespoons butter
1 lb (500 g) callaloo or fresh spinach, washed and dried, tough stems discarded
1 plantain
2 cho-chos (chayote) or 1 zucchini, sliced
2 carrots, peeled and sliced
1 yellow squash, sliced
2 lbs (1 kg) beef tenderloin, cut into 4–6 steaks
12 oz (350 g) cooked fresh or canned ackee
6 sprigs fresh thyme or 1 tablespoon dried thyme

1 Pour 2 tablespoons of the olive oil into a large saucepan. Add the onion and garlic, and sauté until tender, about 5 minutes. Add $\frac{1}{2}$ cup (125 ml) of the red wine to the pan and cook until the liquid is reduced, about 3 to 5 minutes. Add the beef stock and continue to cook until the stock has reduced to a gravy, about 20 minutes. Strain the stock into a small saucepan through a fine sieve and season with salt and pepper. Whisk in 1 tablespoon of the butter and set over low heat to keep warm. Discard the solids.
2 Blanch the callaloo in boiling salted water, drain and set aside. In a small skillet, heat the remaining olive oil over medium heat. Peel and slice the plantains, add them to the pan, and sauté until golden. Remove from the skillet, drain on paper towels and set aside.
3 Blanch all of the sliced vegetables in boiling water, then plunge them in a bowl of ice water to stop the cooking process.
4 Preheat the oven to 400°F (200°C). Heat a large skillet over high heat and sear the steaks on both sides. Put the steaks in the oven and continue cooking until desired doneness. Remove the steaks from the oven and let them stand for 5 minutes before cutting.
5 Heat the remaining butter and wine in a large skillet over medium heat and add all of the blanched vegetables. Cook until heated through, season with salt and pepper and arrange on the plate with the plantains.
6 For a dramatic presentation, build the tower on a dinner plate by cutting each tenderloin crosswise into 3 pieces with a very sharp knife, then layer the beef with ackee and callaloo sandwiched between the 3 pieces as shown. Serve with the warm stock spooned over the top and garnished with fresh thyme.

Serves 6   Cooking time: 1 hour   Preparation time: 1 hour

Garlic Lime Pork Tenderloin with Grilled Pineapple

This festive dish brings together the tangy zest of lime-marinated pork and sweet, juicy pineapple.

2 lbs (1 kg) pork tenderloin, trimmed
1/2 fresh pineapple, peeled, cored and sliced or 6 slices canned pineapple

Marinade
6 cloves garlic
2 tablespoons soy sauce
2 in (5 cm) fresh ginger, peeled and sliced
1/3 cup (90 ml) fresh lime juice
3 tablespoons olive oil

1 To make the Marinade, combine the ingredients in a blender or food processor and pulse until the garlic and ginger are well ground. Pour the Marinade into a zip-lock plastic bag and add the pork. Seal and place in the refrigerator to marinate for at least 4 hours or overnight.
2 Remove the pork from the Marinade and cook on a hot grill or under a preheated broiler for 20 to 25 minutes until cooked through, turning every 5 minutes. Transfer the pork to a platter and let it stand for 5 minutes.
3 Brush any bits of pork from the grill rack and grill the pineapple slices until golden brown, about 2 minutes per side.
4 Slice the pork tenderloin and serve with warm grilled pineapple slices and blanched green beans.

Serves 4 to 6   Preparation time: 5 mins + marination time   Cooking time: 30 mins

Spicy Meat Pies

These spicy meat pies, or "patties", originated in Haiti—but no Jamaican worth his or her Red Stripe will let on that they're made better anywhere else on earth than in Jamaica. The addition of curry is a contribution from Indian immigrants. This delicious version is from Thomas Swan of the Grand Lido Negril.

Pastry
2 cups (300 g) flour
1 1/2 teaspoons curry powder
1/2 teaspoon salt
4 oz (125 g) butter or shortening
Ice water

Filling
1 medium onion, diced
2 spring onions, sliced
1 scotch bonnet or jalapeño chili, deseeded
3/4 lb (350 g) ground beef
1 tablespoon oil
3/4 cup (30 g) unseasoned bread crumbs
1/2 teaspoon dried thyme
1 teaspoon curry powder
Salt and freshly ground black pepper
1/2 cup (125 ml) water

1 Prepare the Pastry by sifting together the flour, curry powder, and salt into a bowl. Add the butter or shortening and combine, using a pastry blender or your fingers, until the mixture resembles a coarse meal. Add just enough ice water to hold the dough together. Mold into a ball, wrap in plastic wrap and refrigerate for at least 1 hour.
2 Prepare the Filling by combining the onion, spring onion, chili and ground beef in a bowl. Heat the oil in a skillet over medium heat. Add the meat mixture, and cook, stirring occasionally, until browned, about 10 minutes. Stir in the remaining ingredients, cover and simmer for 15 to 20 minutes. Remove from the heat and set aside to cool completely.
3 About 15 minutes before assembling the pies, remove the Pastry from the refrigerator and roll out to 1/4 in (6 mm) thickness on a lightly floured board. Using a biscuit or cookie cutter, cut the dough into 12 circles and sprinkle with a bit of flour. Cover with a damp cloth or paper towel.
4 Preheat the oven to 400°F (200°C). Top one half of each Pastry circle with one twelfth of the Filling, fold the other half of the Pastry over it and seal by pressing the edges together with a fork. Place the pies on 2 baking sheets and bake until golden brown, about 30 minutes.

Note: For a vegetarian filling, substitute 2 cups (130 g) cooked, mashed gungo peas or pigeon peas, for the ground beef. Sauté the onion and chili in the oil until translucent, then add the mashed peas with the remaining ingredients and cook for 10 minutes. Add a bit of chicken stock if the mixture is too dry. Set aside to cool and proceed with Step 3 of the recipe.

Makes 12 pies   Preparation time: 45 mins + 1 hour inactive preparation
Cooking time: 1 hour 10 mins

Sunday Roast Beef

This roast from Wayne Lemonious at the Grand Lido Sans Souci has a dark, rich gravy made pungent by scotch bonnet chilies and Pickapeppa sauce.

2$^1/_2$–3 lbs (1$^1/_4$–1$^1/_2$ kg) boneless beef roast, tied
4 teaspoons salt
1 teaspoon freshly ground black pepper
1 teaspoon fresh thyme or $^1/_2$ teaspoon dried thyme
2 spring onions, sliced
2 scotch bonnet or jalapeño chilies, minced
2 cloves garlic, minced
2 tablespoons Pickapeppa sauce or steak sauce
2 tablespoons oil
$^1/_2$ cup (125 ml) water

1 Make small cuts, randomly, all over the surface of the roast. Combine the salt, pepper, thyme, spring onions, chilies, garlic and Pickapeppa in a small bowl. Fill the openings in the beef with the seasoning mixture. Tie the roast in a roll with a kitchen string. Cover the roast and refrigerate overnight.
2 Heat a Dutch oven or a heavy-duty roasting pan over medium-high heat and add the oil. Add the beef and sear on all sides. Add the water and simmer, covered, for 1$^1/_2$ to 2 hours until the beef is cooked (a fork should slide in easily). Add small amounts of water throughout the cooking process, to keep the pan juices from evaporating.
3 Remove the roast from the pan, cut the string, and slice. Serve with the pan juices and Pan-fried Yams (see below).

Serves 8–10   Preparation time: 10 mins + overnight to season
Cooking time: 1$^1/_2$–2 hours

Pan-fried Yams

4 large yams
4 tablespoons oil
4 oz (125 g) butter
Salt

1 Preheat the oven to 400°F (200°C). Make small cuts in the yams to vent steam during cooking, and brush lightly with 1 tablespoon of the oil. Bake in the oven for 25 minutes. Remove from the oven and set aside to cool slightly. Slice into rounds.
2 Melt the butter in a large skillet over medium-high heat. Add the remaining oil and swirl the pan to mix. Add the yams and pan-fry until tender and golden brown on both sides, about 10 minutes. Season with the salt and serve hot.

Note: If your pan is not large enough to accommodate all the yams at once, use half the butter and oil to start and pan-fry in 2 batches.

Serves 8   Preparation time: 5 mins   Cooking time: 35 mins

Jerk Pork or Chicken

A spicy, smoky, uniquely Jamaican dish from Dave Parker at the Grand Lido Sans Souci. You can make this recipe your own by experimenting with the spice paste—add a teaspoon of ground cinnamon or a tablespoon of grated ginger for a different flavor. Create your own secret recipe!

5 lbs (2^1/$_2$ kg) pork loin chops or pork ribs or 2 fresh chickens, quartered

Spice Paste
^{1}/$_3$ cup (20 g) allspice berries or 1 tablespoon ground allspice
7 spring onions, sliced
3 scotch bonnet or jalapeño chilies
3 cloves garlic
4 sprigs fresh thyme, leaves only
5 fresh or 2 dried bay leaves
Salt and freshly ground black pepper

Jerk Sauce
^{1}/$_2$ portion Spice Paste (above)
3 tablespoons freshly grated ginger
3 cups (750 ml) water
3 tablespoons cornstarch dissolved in 3 tablespoons water

1 To prepare the Spice Paste, dry-roast the allspice berries in a small skillet over medium heat for 5 minutes to activate the flavors, then grind them in a mortar or blender until powdery. Place the ground allspice, spring onions, chilies, garlic, thyme, bay leaves, salt and pepper in a food processor and grind to a paste.

2 Place the pork chops or chicken pieces in a large zip-lock plastic bag and cover with the paste. Seal and marinate in the refrigerator overnight.

3 When ready to cook, smoke or bake the seasoned chops in a medium-hot barbecue smoker or in a preheated oven at 350°F (180°C). Cook the pork slowly for 1 hour, turning once. If desired, toss some additional allspice berries or bay leaves onto the coals to add more flavor to the smoke.

4 To make the Jerk Sauce, place the remaining Spice Paste used to marinate the meat, place it in a small saucepan and add the grated ginger and water. Mix well and bring to a boil over high heat. Reduce the heat to low, add the cornstarch mixture and stir until thickened. Serve on the side, if desired.

Note: Chicken and sausage can be jerked with great success using the same spice recipe and the same technique. Cook the chicken on the grill for 40 to 45 minutes until the juices run clear. Cook the sausage for 20 to 30 minutes. Serve with Rice and Peas (page 77) and Pickled Peppers.

Serves 6   Preparation time: 15 mins + marination time   Cooking time: 1 hour

Pickled Peppers

This tangy condiment can be made exclusively with hot peppers like scotch bonnet, jalapeños or Thai bird's eye chilies, or with sweet bell peppers.

8 oz (250 g) mixed peppers, deseeded
2 cups (500 ml) white vinegar
6 allspice berries
^{1}/$_2$ teaspoon salt
^{1}/$_4$ cup (50 g) sugar
1 small onion, thinly sliced

1 Cut the large peppers into pieces and leave the small peppers whole.

2 Combine the vinegar, allspice berries, salt and sugar in a saucepan. Add the peppers and onion, and bring to a boil over high heat. Reduce the heat and simmer for 5 minutes. Set aside to cool.

3 Store the peppers in a glass jar and steep for two days before using.

Preparation time: 10 mins + 2 days to pickle   Cooking time: 5 mins

Bamboo salt and pepper shakers, and jug from Living Wood.

Roasted Cornish Hens with Thyme

This fabulous recipe from Norma Shirley of Norma at the Wharfhouse uses a savory marinade and a sauce of pan juices to make these delicate cornish hens moist and tender.

2 cornish hens or 1 roasting chicken
  (2$^1/_2$ lbs/1$^1/_4$ kg total)
2 large limes, halved
$^1/_2$ cup (125 ml) dry white wine
Fresh thyme springs, to garnish

Marinade
1 small onion, peeled and sliced
3 cloves garlic
1 teaspoon fresh thyme leaves
Salt and freshly ground black pepper
3 tablespoons oil
1 tablespoon cider vinegar
1 teaspoon prepared hot mustard
1 teaspoon fresh lemon or lime juice

1 Rinse the cornish hens or chicken under cold running water, pat them dry, and rub them with the limes, squeezing the juice onto the skin.
2 To make the Marinade, place the onion, garlic, thyme, salt, pepper, oil, vinegar, mustard and lemon or lime juice in a blender or food processor and blend until the onion is minced. Place the hens or chicken in a roasting pan and pour the Marinade over them, using your hands to coat them evenly. Cover and marinate in the refrigerator for at least 2 hours, or overnight.
3 Preheat the oven to 400°F (200°C). Roast the hens for 15 minutes. Reduce the heat to 350°F (175°C) and roast until the juices run clear, about 45 minutes until the chicken is tender and no longer pink. Remove the hens from the pan and set aside.
4 Deglaze the pan with the wine, stirring to create a sauce. Serve the hens hot with the pan juices and with Roasted Sweet Potatoes and Shallots.

Serves 4   Preparation time: 15 mins + marination time   Cooking time: 1 hour

Roasted Sweet Potatoes and Shallots

2–3 sweet potatoes, peeled and cut
  into wedges
3 shallots, peeled and sliced
1 tablespoon olive oil
Pinch each salt and freshly ground
  black pepper

1 Preheat the oven to 400°F (200°C). Line a baking sheet with aluminum foil.
2 Arrange the potato wedges and shallot in a single layer on the baking sheet. Drizzle with the olive oil and sprinkle with salt and pepper. Roast the potatoes for 20 minutes until they are cooked through. Serve warm.

Serves 2 to 4   Preparation time: 5 mins   Cooking time: 20 mins

Napkin from The Craft Cottage.

Ginger Tamarind Chicken

The tangy combination of ginger and tamarind infuse this slow-cooked chicken dish from Noel Coward of Firefly. Rice and Peas make a wonderful side to soak up the tasty sauce.

5 lbs (2¹/₂ kg) chicken pieces
¹/₂ cup (125 ml) fresh lemon or
   lime juice
4 tablespoons oil
3 cloves garlic, minced
2 medium onions, sliced
1 tablespoon freshly grated ginger
2 cups (500 ml) tamarind juice
1 cup (250 ml) water
Salt and freshly ground black pepper

1 Rub the chicken with the lemon or lime juice. Heat the oil in a Dutch oven over medium heat and brown the chicken pieces in batches. Remove the chicken, reduce the heat to medium-low, and add the garlic and onions. Cook until translucent, about 5 minutes. Stir in the ginger.
2 Add the tamarind juice and water, and season with salt and pepper. Return the chicken to the pan, bring to a boil, cover and simmer until the chicken is tender, about 1 hour.

Serves 6–8   Preparation time: 10 mins   Cooking time: 1¹/₂ hours

Rice and Peas

This versatile side can be served with any main dish (photo on page 65).

1 cup (200 g) dried kidney beans,
   soaked overnight
4 cups (1 liter) coconut milk
1 clove garlic, minced
2 spring onions, thinly sliced
1 teaspoon minced fresh thyme leaves
   or ¹/₂ teaspoon dried thyme
3 cups (300 g) uncooked rice,
   washed and drained
2 cups (500 ml) water
2 teaspoons salt
1 tablespoon sugar

1 Drain the soaked peas and combine them with the coconut milk in a medium saucepan. Cook, covered, over medium heat until the beans are tender but not mushy, about 1 hour.
2 Add the remaining ingredients and cook, covered, until the rice absorbs all the liquid, about 15 minutes.

Serves 6–8   Preparation time: 5 mins + overnight to soak the beans
Cooking time: 1 hour 15 mins

Table linens from Patoo Gallery.

Fricasseed Chicken

This Jamaican favorite has many variations—this version is from Norma Shirley of Norma at the Wharfhouse. Create your own with whatever variety of vegetables you happen to have on hand.

1 large chicken (about 3 lbs/$1\frac{1}{2}$ kg), cut into serving pieces
1 tablespoon salt
1 teaspoon sugar
1 teaspoon freshly ground black pepper
1 scotch bonnet chili, minced
4 cloves garlic, minced
3 spring onions, thinly sliced
2 sprigs fresh thyme leaves or 1 teaspoon dried thyme
2 tablespoons oil
2 large onions, diced
2 cups (500 ml) chicken stock or water
1 tablespoon Pickapeppa sauce or steak sauce
$1\frac{1}{2}$ tablespoons tomato ketchup
2 medium potatoes, peeled and cubed
3 carrots, peeled and diced
1 medium cho-cho (chayote) or zucchini, diced

1 Season the chicken with the salt, sugar, pepper, chili, garlic, spring onions and thyme leaves.
2 Heat the oil in a large skillet over medium heat and brown the chicken on both sides. Add the onions and sauté until they are lightly browned. Add the stock or water, Pickapeppa and tomato ketchup. Bring to a boil, reduce the heat, cover and cook for 15 minutes.
3 Add the vegetables and simmer, uncovered, for 20 minutes over medium heat until the chicken and vegetables are tender, stirring occasionally. Serve hot with the pan juices and rice.

Serves 4–6   Preparation time: 25 mins   Cooking time: 50 mins

Wooden rice bowls and plates from Patoo Gallery.

Chicken Roti Roll-ups

Here again is a dish inspired by Jamaica's Indian population—this version is from James Palmer at Strawberry Hill. The Roti Flatbread is stuffed with a spicy curry and cool fresh vegetables.

Chicken Curry
2 tablespoons oil
1 medium onion, diced
4 cloves garlic, minced
1 scotch bonnet or jalapeño chili,
  deseeded and minced
6 tablespoons curry powder
1 chicken (about 2 lbs/1 kg), cut into
  serving pieces
4 cups (1 liter) water

Roti Flatbread
3 cups (450 g) flour
3 tablespoons baking powder
$1/2$ teaspoon salt
1 cup (250 ml) water
Oil, for cooking

Accompaniments
1 avocado, peeled, pitted and sliced
1 small ripe tomato, sliced
$1/2$ cucumber, peeled and sliced
Fresh lime juice
Hot sauce

1 To prepare the Chicken Curry, heat the oil in a Dutch oven or pot over medium heat. Add the onion, garlic and chili and sauté until tender, about 5 minutes. Add the curry powder and mix well. Add the chicken and cook for 4 minutes, stirring occasionally.

2 Add the water, reduce the heat to low, cover and simmer until the chicken is tender, about 30 minutes. Uncover and simmer for another 15 minutes to thicken the sauce. Remove the chicken from the pan and cut the meat off the bone. Continue cooking the sauce, then return the meat to the pan. Stir and heat through.

3 To prepare the Roti Flatbread, sift the flour, baking powder and salt together into a large bowl. Add the water and mix to form a dough. Knead the dough on a lightly-floured surface and let stand, covered, for 30 minutes. Knead the dough again and divide it into 4 balls. Roll out 1 ball as thinly as possible on a floured surface, to a diameter of 8–10 in (20–25 cm).

4 Heat 1 tablespoon oil in a large skillet over medium heat. Add one round of dough and cook about $1^1/_2$ minutes per side, drizzling a little bit of oil on each side as it cooks. Remove the *roti* carefully from the pan and drain on paper towels. Repeat with the remaining rounds of dough.

5 Spoon the curried chicken onto the Roti Flatbread, roll up and serve warm, with avocado, tomato and cucumber slices, a squeeze of fresh lime juice and a dash of hot sauce.

Serves 6–8   Preparation time: 30 mins + 30 mins for Roti Bread dough to rise
Cooking time: 1 hour 5 mins

Red Stripe Chicken

Red Stripe beer and coconut milk lend a distinctive flavor to this dish inspired from Winsome Warren at Jake's Village. Although any beer will work in this recipe, it deserves its name only when you pour on the Red Stripe.

3 tablespoons oil
1 large chicken (about 3 lbs/1¹/₂ kg), cut into serving pieces
2 cups (500 ml) coconut milk
1 cup (250 ml) beer
1 onion, diced
1 large green bell pepper, deseeded and minced
Salt and freshly ground black pepper

1 Heat the oil in a large skillet over medium heat and brown the chicken on both sides. Remove the chicken and pour off all but 2 tablespoons of the oil. Return the chicken to the skillet and add the coconut milk and beer. Bring to a boil, reduce the heat, cover and simmer until almost tender, about 30 minutes.
2 Add the onion and bell pepper, and season with salt and pepper. Simmer, uncovered, until the liquid has been reduced to a gravy, about 15 minutes. If the liquid evaporates before the chicken is done, add more beer or water.

Serves 4–6   Preparation time: 10 mins   Cooking time: 1 hour

Soy Ginger Chicken

Soy sauce, ginger and brown sugar are combined to make a sweet glaze for this one-pot dish of chicken and vegetables.

1 large chicken (about 3 lbs/1¹/₂ kg), cut into serving pieces
1 large onion, diced
4 cloves garlic, minced
¹/₂ cup (125 ml) soy sauce
1 green bell pepper, deseeded and minced
1 red bell pepper, deseeded and minced
¹/₂ cup (60 g) cornstarch
1 tablespoon freshly grated ginger
6 tablespoons brown sugar
2¹/₂ cups (625 ml) chicken stock

1 Preheat the oven to 400°F (220°C). Place the chicken pieces in a small baking pan and season them with the onion, garlic and ¹/₄ cup (60 ml) of the soy sauce. Add the green and red bell pepper to the pan and cover with foil. Bake the chicken for 15 minutes, remove the foil and continue baking until the chicken is light brown, about 15 minutes more.
2 Remove the chicken from the oven and pour the pan juices into a bowl. Add the remaining soy sauce, cornstarch, ginger, brown sugar and chicken stock to the bowl. Pour the mixture over the chicken and bake for an additional 15 minutes until the juices run clear.

Serves 4   Preparation time: 20 mins   Cooking time: 45 mins

Four Bean Salad

Served as a light lunch or a side, these easy and inexpensive recipes from James Palmer of Strawberry Hill, reflects the I-tal vegetarian cuisine of the Rastafarians in Jamaica.

1 cup (100 g) cooked fava beans
1 cup (60 g) cooked or canned kidney beans
1 cup (180 g) cooked green beans
1 cup (180 g) cooked yellow (wax) beans
$^3/_4$ cup (185 ml) freshly squeezed lime juice
Fresh mint leaves, to garnish

1 Mix all the beans together in a large bowl. Pour the lime juice over the top and toss lightly to coat evenly.
2 Cover and marinate in the refrigerator for at least 2 hours. Garnish with the mint leaves and serve.

Serves 6   Preparation time: 10 mins + marination time

Vegetable Stew

This healthy stew can be made with whatever vegetables you may have on hand—butternut squash and zucchini are nice additions.

2 large ripe tomatoes, diced
2 medium potatoes, peeled and diced
1 medium sweet potato, peeled and diced
3 medium carrots, peeled and sliced
2 medium onions, diced
12 oz (350 g) bok choy, callaloo or spinach, washed, dried and sliced
2 spring onions, sliced
6 cups ($1^1/_2$ liters) vegetable stock or water
1 teaspoon fresh thyme leaves or $^1/_2$ teaspoon dried thyme

Place all of the vegetables in a large stockpot, add the stock or water and thyme. Bring to a boil over high heat, then reduce the heat to medium and simmer until the potatoes are tender, about 20 minutes.

Serves 6   Preparation time: 20 mins   Cooking time: 25 mins

Salad set from the Craft Cottage; bowl from Patoo Gallery;
large wooden bowl and fabric from the Strawberry Hill Gift Shop.

Spinach Salad with Breadfruit Chips

This combination of tangy spinach salad with breadfruit or potato chips—a wonderful recipe from the Terra Nova in Kingston—is a great way to kick off a Jamaican meal.

Spinach Salad
1 lb (500 g) fresh spinach, washed
  and dried, tough stems discarded
1 teaspoon salt
1 teaspoon oil
1 medium onion, sliced
6 spring onions, thinly sliced
2 tablespoons lemon juice
2 tablespoons olive oil

Breadfruit Chips
1 green to semi-ripe breadfruit,
  or 3 large potatoes
Heavily salted water
Oil, for frying

1 To prepare the Spinach Salad, tear the spinach into large pieces and place in a large, shallow dish. Sprinkle with the salt and set aside for 15 minutes.
2 Meanwhile, heat the oil in a skillet over medium heat. Add the onion and sauté until tender and translucent, about 5 minutes. Set aside.
3 Drain the spinach, squeeze dry, and place the leaves in a serving bowl. Add the spring onions, lemon juice and olive oil. Toss lightly and garnish with the sautéed onion.
4 To prepare the Breadfruit Chips, peel the breadfruit, cut it into quarters, and remove the core. Slice lengthwise into thick wedges and soak for 1 hour in the salted water. Remove the slices from the water and pat dry with paper towels. If using potatoes, peel and cut into wedges.
5 Heat enough oil to cover the bottom of a large skillet over medium-high heat, until very hot, but not smoking. Fry the breadfruit slices or potato wedges a few at a time until golden brown, about 3 to 5 minutes. Drain on paper towels and salt lightly, if desired. Serve with the Spinach Salad.

Note: The breadfruit or potato chips can also be baked. Follow the same procedure in Step 4 and arrange the slices on a large baking sheet and bake at 375°F (190°C) until tender, about 20 minutes.

Serves 6   Preparation time: 30 mins + 1 hour inactive prep   Cooking time: 20 mins

Leaf platter from The Craft Cottage.

Callaloo Quiche

Delicious island taro greens known locally as callaloo turn this classic European dish into a Caribbean favorite. This version is from Good Hope Plantation Great House.

1 teaspoon oil
12 oz (350 g) callaloo or spinach, washed and dried, tough stems discarded
1 tablespoon butter
1 medium onion, diced
3 large eggs, lightly beaten
2 cups (500 ml) milk
2 scotch bonnet or jalapeño chilies, deseeded and minced
$^1/_2$ teaspoon salt
Pinch of freshly ground black pepper
4 oz (125 g) cheddar cheese
9 in (23 cm) Pie Crust (page 26), unbaked
1 red bell pepper, deseeded and cut into strips

1 Prepare the Pie Crust by following the instructions on page 26.
2 Preheat the oven to 425°F (220°C). Heat the oil in a skillet over medium heat. Add the callaloo or spinach and sauté until just wilted, about 3 to 5 minutes. Remove from the skillet and set aside.
3 Return the skillet to the stove, melt the butter over medium heat, and sauté the onion until tender, about 5 minutes. Add the eggs, milk, callaloo or spinach, chilies, salt and pepper, and mix well.
4 Sprinkle half the cheese into the Pie Crust. Pour the filling into the Pie Crust and sprinkle the remaining cheese over the top. Arrange the strips of red bell pepper on top and bake for 30 to 35 minutes until a knife inserted in the center comes out clean.

Serves 6–8   Preparation time: 15 mins   Cooking time: 45 mins

Ceramic platter, wooden table and chairs by David Pinto.

Stuffed Plantain Boats

Ripe plantains stuffed with a hearty filling and topped with cheese. Ham or bacon can be substituted for the ground pork. For a vegetarian version, use beans and pumpkin or butternut squash in place of the meat.

2 lbs (1 kg) plantains, about 6 ripe and firm plantains or 8 large unripe bananas
$^1/_2$ cup (125 ml) oil
$^1/_2$ cup (50 g) finely grated cheddar cheese

Filling
2 tablespoons olive oil
1 tablespoon butter
1 scotch bonnet or jalapeño chili, deseeded and minced
2 cloves garlic, minced
$^1/_2$ red bell pepper, deseeded and minced
$^1/_2$ green bell pepper, deseeded and minced
8 oz (250 g) ground pork
3 spring onions, green and white parts, thinly sliced
Salt and freshly ground black pepper

1 To make the Filling, heat the oil and butter in a large skillet over medium heat. Add the scotch bonnet chili and garlic, and sauté for 30 seconds. Add the bell peppers and sauté for 4 minutes until soft. Add the pork and sauté until the pork is cooked, about 5 minutes. Add the spring onions and season with salt and pepper. Set aside.
2 Peel the plantains or bananas. Heat the oil in a large skillet over medium-high heat until hot but not smoking. Fry the plantains until golden brown, about 2 minutes per side. Remove and drain on paper towels.
3 Preheat the oven to 350°F (175°C). Make a slit in each plantain from top to bottom. Fill each plantain with 3 tablespoons of the Filling and sprinkle with a bit of the cheese. Place on a foil-lined baking sheet and bake for 15 minutes until heated through.

Serves 6   Preparation time: 15 mins   Cooking time: 30 mins

Plantain Tarts

This recipe of sweetened, spiced plantains from Clifton Wright at the Grand Lido Negril, make a tasty tart filling for these flaky pastries. Freshly grated nutmeg gives a wonderful spicy fragrance to these tarts—but if you cannot find whole nutmegs, you may use ground nutmeg instead.

Pastry
2 cups (300 g) flour
8 oz (250 g) vegetable shortening
1 teaspoon ground cinnamon
$1/4$ teaspoon freshly grated nutmeg
  or ground nutmeg
$1/4$ teaspoon salt
About 2 tablespoons ice water

Filling
1 large very ripe plantain or banana,
  mashed
$1/2$ cup (125 g) sugar
1 tablespoon unsalted butter
$1/2$ teaspoon freshly grated nutmeg
  or ground nutmeg
1 teaspoon vanilla extract
1 tablespoon raisins

1 To make the Pastry, combine half the flour with the shortening in a bowl and cut in with a pastry blender until the mixture resembles peas. Add the remaining flour, cinnamon, nutmeg and salt, and cut again until the mixture resembles bread crumbs. Add enough ice water to hold the mixture together, form into a ball, wrap in plastic wrap and refrigerate for 1 hour until firm.
2 To make the Filling, combine the mashed plantain, sugar and butter in a saucepan. Cook over medium heat until the mixture is thoroughly blended and the butter is melted, about 5 minutes. Stir in the nutmeg, vanilla and raisins, and set aside to cool.
3 Preheat the oven to 450°F (230°C). Roll out the pastry on a lightly floured surface to a thickness of $1/8$ in (3 mm). Using a drinking glass, cut the pastry into 4 in (10 cm) circles. Spoon about 2 teaspoons of the Filling in the center of each. Fold the pastry in half over the Filling and seal by crimping the edges with a fork.
4 Place the tarts on a baking sheet lined with parchment paper. Prick the top of each with a fork to vent steam and bake until the pastry is light brown, about 15 minutes.

Makes about 40 small tarts   Preparation time: 30 mins + 1 hour refrigeration
Cooking time: 20 mins

Leaf platters from The Craft Cottage.

Crunchy Banana Bread with Peanuts

The sweetness of ripe bananas blended with crunchy peanuts make this banana bread from Good Hope Plantation Great House a comforting dessert or a satisfying snack.

4 oz (125 g) unsalted butter, softened
$^1/_2$ cup (100 g) packed light brown sugar
3 egg yolks
2 cups (300 g) flour
1 teaspoon ground cloves
1 tablespoon baking powder
Pinch of salt
2 very ripe bananas, mashed
1 teaspoon vanilla extract
$^1/_2$ cup (60 g) chopped peanuts

1 Preheat the oven to 325°F (160°C). Grease a loaf pan and set it aside. In a medium bowl, cream the butter and sugar until light and fluffy. Add the egg yolks and mix thoroughly.
2 In a separate bowl, sift together the flour, cloves, baking powder and salt.
3 Combine the mashed banana and vanilla in a small bowl and add this, a little at a time, to the egg-butter mixture, alternating with additions of sifted dry ingredients. Mix until just combined, then fold in the peanuts.
4 Pour the batter into the prepared pan and bake for 1 hour until a toothpick inserted in the center comes out clean. Cool on a wire rack for 10 minutes. Remove from the loaf pan and cool completely on the rack.

Makes 1 loaf   Preparation time: 20 mins   Cooking time: 1 hour

Banana Fritters

The sweetness of bananas lightly battered, fried until golden and then dusted with sugar makes a satisfying snack or a tasty ending to a meal.

$^1/_3$ cup (50 g) flour
$^1/_2$ teaspoon baking powder
Pinch of salt
4 ripe bananas, mashed
1 teaspoon fresh lime juice
1 large egg
3 tablespoons sugar
4 tablespoons oil
Confectionery sugar, to garnish

1 Combine the flour, baking powder and salt in a small bowl. In a separate bowl, combine the mashed bananas and lime juice.
2 Beat the egg and the sugar in a large bowl; stir in the bananas and then the flour mixture.
3 Heat the oil in a large skillet over medium-high heat. Gently drop the batter, a few heaping tablespoons at a time, in the hot oil. Fry the fritters until brown and crisp, about 3 minutes, then drain on paper towels. Serve warm, sprinkled with confectionary sugar.

Serves 6   Preparation time: 15 mins   Cooking time: 10 mins

Ceramics by David Pinto.

Tropical Fruit Mousse

A light, refreshing dessert from Dennis McIntosh at Ciboney can be made with almost any tropical fruit juice.

6 tablespoons cornstarch
1 cup (250 ml) unsweetened pineapple juice
1 cup (250 ml) fresh or canned mango juice
1/2 cup (125 g) sugar
1 cup (250 ml) unsweetened whipped cream

1 Dissolve the cornstarch in a bit of the pineapple juice. Pour the remaining juice and mango juice into a saucepan and heat over high heat.
2 Add the sugar and dissolved cornstarch and bring to a boil. Reduce the heat to medium and simmer, stirring constantly, for 5 minutes until the mixture thickens. Remove from the heat and cool completely.
3 Fold the whipped cream into the cooled juice mixture. Spoon into 6 individual serving dishes and refrigerate until chilled.

Serves 6   Preparation time: 5 mins   Cooking time: 5 mins

Sweet Potato Pone

This particular pone, similar to those found in the Southern part of the United States, was inspired by the rich culinary heritage of Africa. This recipe is from Dennis McIntosh at Ciboney.

2 lbs (1 kg) sweet potatoes, peeled and sliced
2 tablespoons brown sugar
2 oz (60 g) butter
1/4 cup (60 ml) orange juice
2 large eggs, separated
1/2 cup (125 ml) dark rum
1/4 teaspoon salt

1 Cook the sweet potatoes in boiling water for 20 minutes until tender. Drain and mash the potatoes with the brown sugar and butter. Stir in the orange juice. Lightly beat the egg yolks and add them to the sweet potato mixture along with the rum.
2 Preheat the oven to 350°F (175°C). Grease a pie plate or baking dish and set it aside.
3 Beat the egg whites with the salt until stiff but not dry. Gently fold the egg whites into the potato mixture. Pour into the prepared dish and bake for 30 minutes until a knife inserted in the center comes out clean.

Serves 6–8   Preparation time: 10 mins   Cooking time: 50 mins

Cake plate from The Craft Cottage.

Coconut Pecan Drops

These deliciously chewy nuggets are made of coconut, pecans (or almonds), brown sugar and freshly grated ginger. Both of these recipes are from Clifton Wright at Grand Lido Negril.

2 cups (500 ml) water
2 cups (150) unsweetened
  dried coconut
1 tablespoon freshly grated ginger
2 cups (400 g) packed brown sugar
$1/4$ cup (30 g) pecans or almonds,
  coarsely chopped

1 Grease a baking sheet and set it aside. Bring the water to a boil in a heavy saucepan over high heat. Add the coconut and ginger, reduce the heat to medium and cook for 15 minutes.
2 Gradually add the sugar, stirring to dissolve it. Increase the heat to high and cook the mixture until it is thick and sticky, about 20 to 30 minutes, stirring frequently. Drop a little bit of the mixture into a glass of cold water. If it turns into a ball, it's done. Turn off the heat and stir in the nuts.
3 Using a greased teaspoon, drop the mixture onto the prepared baking sheet and let the candies cool.

Makes 20 large drops   Preparation time: 15 mins   Cooking time: 45 mins

Gizadas

Tender, short crust pastries filled with a sweet coconut filling.

1 cup (150 g) fresh or dried unsweetened grated coconut
$2/3$ cup (140 g) packed brown sugar
$1/2$ teaspoon freshly grated nutmeg
  or ground nutmeg
1 portion Pie Crust (page 26), chilled

1 Prepare the Pie Crust by following the instructions on page 26.
2 Preheat the oven to 375°F (190°C). Grease a baking sheet and set it aside.
3 Combine the coconut, brown sugar and nutmeg in a bowl. Pinch off small pieces of the Pie Crust dough and roll each piece into a 3 in ($7^1/_2$ cm) circle on a lightly floured surface.
4 Pinch up the edge of a circle of dough to form a ridge and fill with 2 to 3 tablespoons of the coconut mixture. Set on the prepared baking sheet and repeat with the remaining circles of dough.
5 Bake the tarts until golden brown, about 20 minutes. Cool on a wire rack.

Makes 12–14 tarts   Preparation time: 20 mins   Cooking time: 20 mins

Background painting and glass plates
from Magic Kitchen.

Otaheiti Apples Poached in Wine

Fresh fruit is always the perfect ending to a meal. This classic European dessert from Norma Shirley of Norma at the Wharfhouse is given a tropical twist with delicate otaheiti apples. If you can't find otaheiti apples, you can substitute fresh pears.

6 peeled otaheiti apples or ripe pears, peeled
3 cups (750 ml) water
1 cup (250 ml) dry red wine
1$\frac{1}{2}$ cups (300 g) sugar
1 cinnamon stick
Rind of 1 lime
Rind of 1 orange
1 cup (250 ml) coconut cream

1 Place the apples or pears in a large saucepan. Add all the ingredients, except the coconut cream, and bring to a boil over high heat. Reduce the heat to low and simmer until the flesh is cooked but firm, 8 to 10 minutes. Take care not to overcook the fruit or it will fall apart.
2 Remove the apples from the pan and continue to simmer the liquid until it is reduced to syrup. Set the syrup aside to cool, then pour over the poached apples. Refrigerate the apples and syrup, and serve chilled with coconut cream drizzled on top.

Serves 6   Preparation time: 5 mins   Cooking time: 15 mins

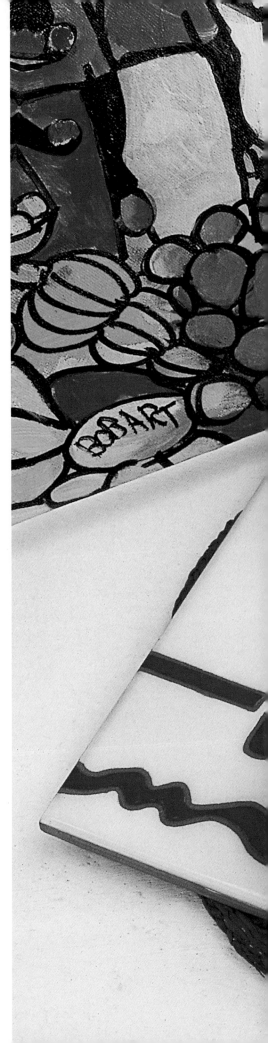

Totoes

Children will love this slightly sweet and spicy cake. Both these recipes are from Dennis McIntosh at Ciboney.

2 cups (300 g) flour
2 teaspoons baking powder
1 teaspoon ground cinnamon
$^1/_2$ teaspoon freshly grated nutmeg or ground nutmeg
4 oz (125 g) unsalted butter, softened
$^1/_2$ cup (100 g) sugar
$^1/_2$ cup (100 g) packed light brown sugar
1 large egg, beaten
2 teaspoons vanilla extract
About $^1/_2$ cup (125 ml) milk

1 Preheat the oven to 375˚F (190˚C). Grease an 8 in (20 cm) round cake pan and set it aside.
2 In a small bowl, combine the flour, baking powder, cinnamon and nutmeg, and set it aside.
3 In a large bowl, cream the butter with the sugars using a hand mixer. Add the egg and vanilla and mix well. Gradually stir in the dry ingredients and enough of the milk to make a thick dough.
4 Spread the batter in the prepared pan and bake for 30 to 35 minutes until golden brown. Cool on a wire rack and cut into wedges.

Serves 9   Preparation time: 20 mins   Cooking time: 35 mins

Gingerbread

$^1/_4$ cup (125 ml) molasses
1 cup (200 g) sugar
4 oz (125 g) butter
$^1/_2$ cup (125 ml) hot water
2 cups (300 g) flour
1 teaspoons baking powder
$^1/_2$ teaspoon salt
1 teaspoon freshly grated nutmeg or ground nutmeg
2 teaspoons freshly grated ginger
1 large egg, beaten

1 Preheat the oven to 300˚F (150˚C). Grease a loaf pan, then line it with waxed paper and set it aside.
2 In a medium saucepan over low heat, heat the molasses, sugar and butter, stirring until the butter is melted. Add the hot water, mix well and set the pan aside.
3 In a bowl, sift together the flour, baking powder, salt and nutmeg. Add the ginger and egg and mix well. Pour the molasses mixture into the flour mixture and stir until just combined. Pour the batter into the prepared pan and bake for 1 hour until a toothpick inserted in the center comes out clean.

Serves 9   Preparation time: 10 mins   Cooking time: 1 hour 5 mins

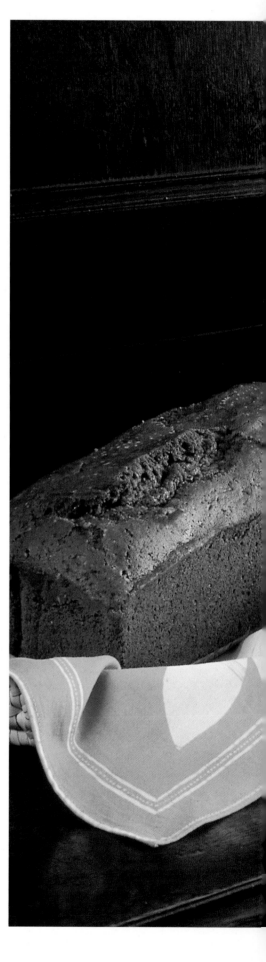

Round wooden cake platter by Tony Barton of A.C.E. Woodwork.

Rum Cake

A traditional favorite at weddings and holidays, this cake is made moist and flavorful by rum-soaked dried fruit. You can experiment by substituting whatever dried or candied fruit you have on hand.

$1^1/_2$ cups (375 ml) dark rum
1 cup (175 g) dates
1 cup (150 g) dried apricots
1 cup (150 g) raisins
1 cup (175 g) dried cherries
4 eggs
$1^3/_4$ cup (350 g) firmly packed
  brown sugar
4 tablespoons molasses
6 oz (180 g) unsalted butter, melted
3 cups (450 g) flour
2 teaspoons baking powder
1 teaspoon salt
2 teaspoons ground cinnamon
$1/_2$ teaspoon freshly grated nutmeg
  or ground nutmeg
$1/_2$ teaspoon ground allspice
$1/_2$ teaspoon ground cloves
2 cups (200 g) pecan halves

1 Combine 1 cup (250 ml) of the rum with all the dried fruit in a large bowl. Set aside for at least 2 hours to soak.
2 Preheat the oven to 275°F (135°C). Grease two loaf pans and line with parchment paper.
3 In a large bowl beat the eggs until foamy. Gradually add the brown sugar, beating until light and fluffy. Add remaining $1/_2$ cup (125 ml) rum, molasses and melted butter, and mix well.
4 In another large bowl sift together the flour, baking powder, salt and ground spices. Add the pecans and rum-soaked fruit and toss gently to coat. Add the egg mixture and mix just enough to incorporate.
5 Divide the batter among the prepared pans and bake for $2^1/_2$ to 3 hours until a toothpick inserted in the center of the cake comes out clean. Cool in the pans, on a rack, for 15 minutes before turning out. Store in an airtight container.

Makes 2 loaves   Preparation time: 20 mins + 2 hours to soak fruit
Baking time: $2^1/_2$ hours

Tropical Fruit Smoothies

Refreshing smoothies can be made by mixing juices and fresh fruits in a blender, along with some fruit syrup and crushed ice. This recipe, as well as those for the tropical cocktails below, is from Grand Lido Negril.

5 cups ($1\frac{1}{2}$ liters) orange juice
2 cups (500 ml) pineapple juice
1 cup (250 ml) guava or mango juice
2 small papayas, peeled and cut into chunks
Juice of 2 limes
3 ripe bananas
1 tablespoon Strawberry Syrup or sugar

Combine all the ingredients in a blender and blend until smooth. Pour over ice and garnish with fruit slices, if desired.

Serves 10   Preparation time: 5 mins

Strawberry Syrup

This all-purpose fruit syrup can be used to sweeten a variety of tropical drinks.

2 cups (360 g) fresh or frozen strawberries
1 cup (200 g) sugar
$^3/_4$ cup (185 ml) light corn syrup
1 tablespoon fresh lemon juice

1 Purée the strawberries in a food processor. Pour the purée into a saucepan and cook, gently stirring, over medium heat until it comes to a boil, about 6 to 8 minutes.
2 Strain the purée into a bowl, pressing on the fruit to extract as much juice as possible. Discard the pulp.
3 Return the juice to the pan and add the sugar and corn syrup. Cook over medium heat until the mixture comes to a boil, about 10 minutes. Boil for 1 minute, add the lemon juice, remove from the heat and set aside to cool. Store refrigerated.

Makes 2 cups (500 ml)   Preparation time: 15 mins   Cooking time: 20 mins

Pineapple Ginger Drink

Peel of 1 fresh pineapple
1 tablespoon freshly grated ginger
3 cups (750 ml) boiling water
Sugar, to taste
Crushed ice

1 Scrub the pineapple well and rinse with water, then peel. Cut the pineapple for serving later, cover and keep in the refrigerator.
2 Place the pineapple peel in a large container with the ginger, then add the boiling water and let steep overnight. Strain the liquid, then sweeten with sugar to taste. Cover and refrigerate until chilled. Serve over crushed ice.

Serves 4   Preparation time: 5 mins + overnight to steep

Carrot Drink

2 medium carrots, peeled
2 cups (500 ml) water
1 cup (250 ml) evaporated milk
$1/2$ cup (100 g) sugar
$1/4$ teaspoon freshly grated nutmeg
  or ground nutmeg
1 teaspoon vanilla extract
4 ice cubes

Place the carrots and water in a blender and blend for 30 seconds. Strain the liquid and rinse the blender. Return the carrot juice to the blender along with the remaining ingredients and blend until thickened. Cover and refrigerate until chilled, then serve.

Serves 6   Preparation time: 10 mins

Beet Drink

2 cups (500 ml) water
2 medium beets, peeled
2 tablespoons sweetened condensed
  milk
$1/4$ teaspoon freshly grated nutmeg
  or ground nutmeg
Crushed ice

Combine the water and beets in a blender and blend until the beets are finely ground. Strain the beets, rinse the blender, and return the beet juice to the blender with the remaining ingredients. Blend for 10 seconds. Cover and refrigerate until chilled. Serve over crushed ice.

Serves 4   Preparation time: 5 mins

Jamaican Limeade

3 tablespoons sugar syrup or
  corn syrup
2 cups (500 ml) water
Juice of 2 large limes
Crushed Ice

Combine the sugar syrup and water in a small pitcher then add the lime juice. Stir and serve over crushed ice.

Serves 2   Preparation time: 5 mins

Tamarind Cooler

Like lemon, tart tamarind juice can punch up the flavor of foods. On its own, it makes a delicious drink.

2 cups (500 ml) seedless tamarind pulp or tamarind concentrate
4 cups (1 liter) water
Sugar syrup or sugar, to taste
Crushed Ice
Sparkling mineral water or soda water (optional)

Combine the tamarind pulp, water and sugar syrup in a blender and blend until smooth. Cover and chill, about 30 minutes. Add sparkling or soda water to thin to desired consistency and serve over crushed ice.

Serves 4   Preparation time: 5 mins

Sorrel Drink

Sorrel is a tropical plant whose red petals are popular in drinks, jams and jellies. Though it is sold fresh in Jamaica at Christmas, it is available dried all year.

1 oz (30 g) dried sorrel petals
1 cinnamon stick
1 piece dried orange peel
6 whole cloves
2 cups (400 g) sugar
8 cups (2 liters) boiling water
4 tablespoons medium dark rum
1 teaspoon ground cinnamon
$^1/_4$ teaspoon ground cloves

1 In a large heatproof jar, combine the sorrel petals, cinnamon stick, orange peel, whole cloves and sugar. Pour in the boiling water. Cover loosely and steep at room temperature for 2 to 3 days.
2 Strain the sorrel mixture, add the rum, ground cinnamon and ground cloves. Cover and refrigerate for an additional 2 days. Strain through a fine sieve lined with cheesecloth. Serve in chilled glasses over ice cubes, if desired.

Makes 8 cups ($2^1/_2$ liters)   Preparation time: 5 mins + 5 days to steep

Soursop Drink

Jamaicans call this drink Nerve Juice because it's said to calm your nerves. Soursop leaves are reputed to have healing properties and are also used for muscle sprains.

$^1/_2$ cup (125 ml) fresh or frozen soursop, peeled, seeds removed
Juice of 1 lime
2 cups (500 ml) water
2 tablespoons sweetened condensed milk
2 tablespoons white rum
Pinch of freshly grated nutmeg or ground nutmeg
Crushed ice

Combine all the ingredients in a blender and blend until smooth. Serve over crushed ice and garnish with additional grated nutmeg.

Serves 2   Preparation time: 5 mins

Caribbean Sky

1¹/₂ oz (45 ml) blue curaçao
2 slices pineapple
¹/₄ cup (60 ml) gold rum
¹/₄ cup (60 ml) lime juice
¹/₄ cup (60 ml) sugar syrup or
  3 tablespoons caster sugar
  dissolved in 3 tablespoons water
2 cups crushed ice

Serves 2
Preparation time: 5 mins

Place all the ingredients in a blender and blend until slushy. Pour into 2 chilled glasses and serve.

Mango Daiquiri

4 tablespoons light rum
1 oz (30 ml) curaçao
¹/₂ fresh ripe mango, peeled and pitted
2 tablespoons lime juice
1 tablespoon caster sugar
2 cups crushed ice

Serves 2
Preparation time: 5 mins

Place all the ingredients in a blender and blend until slushy. Pour into 2 chilled glasses and serve.

Pink Lady

¹/₂ cup (125 ml) evaporated milk
¹/₄ cup (60 ml) Strawberry Syrup
  (page 106)
¹/₄ cup (60 ml) gin
4 ice cubes

Serves 2
Preparation time: 5 mins

Prepare the Strawberry Syrup by following the instructions on page 106. Blend all the ingredients in a blender and strain into 2 glasses.

Yellow Bird

2 tablespoons lime juice
4 teaspoons sugar
¹/₂ cup (125 ml) orange juice
1 tablespoon Tia Maria
¹/₄ cup (60 ml) rum
1 tablespoon crème de banana
²/₃ cup (175 ml) Galliano
4 ice cubes

Serves 1
Preparation time: 5 mins

Blend all the ingredients in a blender and pour into a 12-oz (350-ml) glass. Garnish with fruit.

Complete list of recipes

Measurements and conversions

Measurements in this book are given in volume as far as possible. Teaspoon, tablespoon and cup measurements should be level, not heaped, unless otherwise indicated. Australian readers please note that the standard Australian measuring spoon is larger than the UK or American spoon by 5 ml, so use $3/4$ tablespoon instead of a full tablespoon when following the recipes.

Liquid Conversions

Imperial	Metric	US cups
$1/2$ fl oz	15 ml	1 tablespoon
1 fl oz	30 ml	$1/8$ cup
2 fl oz	60 ml	$1/4$ cup
3 fl oz	85 ml	$1/3$ cup
4 fl oz	125 ml	$1/2$ cup
5 fl oz	150 ml	$2/3$ cup
6 fl oz	175 ml	$3/4$ cup
8 fl oz	250 ml	1 cup
12 fl oz	375 ml	$1 1/2$ cups
16 fl oz	500 ml	2 cups
1 quart	1 liter	4 cups

Note: 1 UK pint = 20 fl oz
1 US pint = 16 fl oz

Solid Weight Conversions

Imperial	Metric
$1/2$ oz	15 g
1 oz	28 g
$1 1/2$ oz	45 g
2 oz	60 g
3 oz	85 g
$3 1/2$ oz	100 g
4 oz ($1/4$ lb)	125 g
5 oz	150 g
6 oz	175 g
7 oz	200 g
8 oz ($1/2$ lb)	225 g
9 oz	260 g
10 oz	300 g
16 oz (1 lb)	450 g
32 oz (2 lbs)	1 kg

Oven Temperatures

Heat	Fahrenheit	Centigrade/Celsius	British Gas Mark
Very cool	230	110	$1/4$
Cool or slow	275–300	135–150	1–2
Moderate	350	175	4
Hot	425	220	7
Very hot	450	230	8